P9-DOF-940

MAYOR *for a* NEW AMERICA

MAYOR *for a* NEW AMERICA

Thomas M. Menino
FORMER FIVE-TERM MAYOR OF BOSTON

with

Jack Beatty

Houghton Mifflin Harcourt
BOSTON NEW YORK
2014

www.hmhco.com

Library of Congress Cataloging-in-Publication Data is available.
ISBN 978-0-544-30249-5

Book design by Brian Moore

Printed in the United States of America
DOC 10 9 8 7 6 5 4 3 2 1

Contents

Introduction

> Nothing can defeat the heart of this city. Nothing. Nothing will take us down because we take care of one another.
>
> —*from my remarks at the interfaith service held at the Cathedral of the Holy Cross in Boston after the Marathon bombing*

"Mayor, we've just had a major explosion at the Marathon!" my security aide, Sergeant Mike Cunnife, shouted from the doorway of my hospital room. "Not one, but two." I flicked on my TV and saw wild footage of racers staggering out of a storm of debris and police running into it. While I watched in horror, an announcer said that an incendiary device had just been detonated at the JFK Library in Dorchester. The news crawl reported that police had found "multiple explosive devices in Boston." *Dear God,* I thought, *how big would this get?* If two bombs (or three), why not ten? If on Boylston Street, why not elsewhere—why not anywhere? If these wounded spectators, the ones who must be sprawled on the sidewalk under the white cloud, why not others lining the route five deep for miles? As the smoke cleared, I caught sight of a Marathon banner on a lamppost with my signature beneath the slogan THIS IS YOUR MOMENT.

The first bomb went off at the finish line across the street from a small grandstand. If I hadn't broken my leg, I would have been sitting there cheering a runner from my staff who crossed the finish line minutes ahead of the blast. With my grandkids. In the front row. A district fire chief, I later learned, sent the bomb squad to search for a possible third unexploded bomb planted *under the grandstand.*

As the first bomb exploded in an endless loop on television, something else came back to me, something my son Tommy, a police detective, had told me in passing. He'd be on Boylston, he said, near the finish line.

A press conference was scheduled for five o'clock at the Westin Hotel. My nurses at Brigham and Women's Hospital had less than two hours to fit me with a walking cast and a catheter. I called Governor Deval Patrick and said if I wasn't there, to start without me. Delay was our enemy. Either public officials would fill the information hole or rumor would.

My doctor advised me to stay put. It was important to keep the leg elevated. (I had a history of blood clots.) It was vital not to put weight on my foot. On Saturday a steel plate had been screwed into my right ankle. This was Monday. Too soon to move, too risky . . .

"I don't care what you say, doc, I'm going," I said. My city had been attacked. I had to be out there.

Dot Joyce, my press secretary, reported that casualties were arriving at the front entrance of the Brigham, and reporters were collecting in the lobby. I couldn't leave that way. Not unless I wanted microphones thrust in my face with victims being stretchered into the ER behind me.

Waiting in the hallway while I dressed, Dot and Mike saw something out the window that took their breath away. Sixteen stories below, police were surrounding a car stopped in the middle of the street. Mike got on his cell. Someone had abandoned the car. Inside was a suspicious package. It was being checked out. Mike would be told when it was safe for me to leave.

That was the atmosphere in Boston. Fear was spreading.

We took the freight elevator to the loading dock at the back of the hospital. Mike and Dot loaded me and my wheelchair into my SUV. Mike pulled out onto Francis Street. As we passed the front of the hospital, TV reporters began frantically gesturing to their cameramen to get a shot of the departing mayor. Mike turned left on Huntington Ave, heading downtown toward the Westin.

The police scanner crackled. The superintendent was redeploying his forces from the Marathon route to historic sites like Faneuil Hall, to the train stations, to the hospitals. Mike flicked on the blue lights. When the traffic knotted, he tapped the siren.

Dot had drafted some remarks for me to deliver. We discussed points to hit. Boston was strong, its people resilient. We would get through this if we stuck together . . . Half-heard words on the radio distracted us. We resumed talking for a few minutes, then the siren went off. The sound was hell on the nerves.

The sunny April day had been warm enough to draw tens of thousands outdoors to watch the race but cool enough so the 23,000 runners did not risk dehydration. The first part of the drive down Huntington, it still looked like the same day outside — Boston Before. We came up on the other side of the short tunnel beneath Mass Ave in Boston After. Lower Huntington had been turned into a staging area for state and city SWAT teams. Gray military-style vehicles lined the street. Black-clad officers were everywhere, automatic rifles slung over their shoulders, muzzles pointing down. It was like entering a war zone. But where was the front? And who was the enemy?

If government didn't act calmly and confidently, I was afraid the solidarity seen by millions after the bombing might fray. Episodes of vigilante violence against strangers had marred the aftermath of

9/11. That must not happen in a Boston teeming with "strangers"—Marathon competitors and fans from everywhere.

I wanted the focus to be on the heroism of the first responders, on the resourcefulness of the nurses who saved lives in medical tents equipped to treat blisters, and on the decency of race watchers who took stranded runners into their homes. Instead of telling that story, I worried that the media would continue to highlight the mayhem and the manhunt. Leaving my room I had heard a TV talking head say, "State and city authorities are treating Boston as a city under attack."

So when security people at the Westin meeting urged the governor to declare a state of emergency, I said that was exactly the wrong thing to do. We needed to reassure citizens that we were taking the right steps to safeguard the city. Not scare the hell out of them. Governor Patrick agreed.

At the press conference, I made my points about the strength and resilience of Boston's people. Within hours Emerson College students had created the hashtag #Boston Strong, and that legend was appearing on T-shirts selling online.

In photographs of the event my head is bowed, as if, in my first quiet moment since the bombs went off, the blow to the city was hitting me for the first time. I remember feeling grief for the dead and injured, and rage at the terrorists who splattered blood on the century-old Boston Marathon. And I was frustrated that at Boston's worst moment I couldn't be at my best.

At a second press conference on Monday evening, I said Boston would be open for business on Tuesday morning: "People returning to work tomorrow will notice an increased police presence in the city. They should not be alarmed." Only the area around Copley Square—"the largest crime scene in Boston's history"—would be closed off.

Leaving the Westin, I asked Mike to drive to the finish line. We got close enough to see FBI and ATF agents picking over the shrapnel, nails, ball bearings, backpacks, duffel bags, and cell phones littering Boylston Street. I didn't realize it then, but the body of eight-year-old Martin Richard still lay on the sidewalk. The police commissioner, Ed Davis, called with that news. He said family members were anxious to remove Martin, but the FBI didn't want the crime scene disturbed. Jesus, I said, can't you hurry them up? "I'll try," he said.

Martin was from Dorchester. I knew his family. I didn't know that his mother, Denise, had been struck in the eye by a ball bearing. Or that his seven-year-old sister, Jane, had lost her left leg.

Martin was one of three spectators near the finish line killed by the blast, the cable channels reported that night. Over two hundred and fifty were wounded. EMTs, police, and firefighters carried them to ambulances, squad cars, and fire trucks, which rushed them to nine hospitals. Many were in critical condition; some had lost limbs, and a few more than one.

Tommy spent Monday afternoon and evening at the Brigham, panning for clues that might lead to the bombers by gently questioning their horribly wounded victims. Senator Elizabeth Warren and I were scheduled to visit some of them on Tuesday. Tommy came upstairs to brace me. "No one should ever see what I saw today," he said.

Elizabeth and I saw young women who seemed to get younger as we went from room to room past grieving loved ones in the hall. Please, I said to the nurses, ask if it's OK for us to come in.

I wanted to apologize for what had happened to them in my city. But stricken people don't want mea culpas. They want help. You learn that talking to parents of murdered kids. Concentrate on your recovery and don't worry about anything else, I said. Caring people from all over the world are contributing to a fund to help you get on with your life as rapidly as possible.

We met one woman who chatted and smiled as if losing a leg was no big deal. She was, we realized, trying to cheer us up.

On Monday night, alone in my room, it came to me: We had to do something for these people. We needed one fund — not five or six — so the money would get out the door quickly. From experience I knew how easily money could get stuck in institutional pipelines dedicated to other uses. To emphasize that it was the only game in town, we called it One Fund Boston. My chief of staff, Mitch Weiss, who'd started up a nonprofit, took the reins with help from the team at City Hall. By five o'clock that afternoon, thanks to Mike Sheehan, the CEO of Hill Holliday, the Boston advertising agency, the One Fund had a logo and was accepting donations through a website.

While we were making these arrangements, I took a phone call from Jim Gallagher, the executive vice president of John Hancock, the chief sponsor of the Boston Marathon, whose tower looms over the finish line and whose employees working the race did yeoman service after the bombing. Jim wanted to know what name to write on Hancock's check for $1 million. I was flabbergasted. I knew how competitive generosity worked. Hancock had set a high bar for the city's other corporate citizens. They — New Balance, State Street Bank & Trust, Bain Capital, the Red Sox, others — promptly hurdled it. Our initial goal was to raise $10 million. The One Fund collected $7.5 million in the first twenty-four hours, and not just from businesses but from nearly ten thousand individuals.

By the close of business on day one, the One Fund had recruited a proven administrator, Ken Feinberg, the former aide to Senator Ted Kennedy, who managed the biggest 9/11 survivors' fund. I called him in New York from my bed.

With contributions from the ninety-two countries that sent runners to the Marathon and from all fifty states, the One Fund raised $61 million between April 16 and July 1 and gave all of it to victims of the bombing. Another $13 million poured in by the end of the year. Contributions ranged from Hancock's million to the $38 in cash raised at a lemonade stand by Kristine and Gwen, who didn't give their address.

The biggest cash gift received by the One Fund was completely anonymous. During the first post-bombing game at Fenway Park, the Red Sox passed the hat among the fans. I stopped by the clubhouse to see the $43,000 haul. A Red Sox executive started to hand me a big bag of money. "No, no, I can't touch that," I protested, picturing the caption under the photograph. Nodding toward David Ortiz, the Red Sox slugger and team character, I said, "Give it to David." Discretion is not Big Papi's game. He swung the bag around his head to heighten the drama. *Oh no,* I yelled, just as he poured the bills and coins onto the floor.

Every one of the 200,000 contributions was precious to us. They showed love for our little city. They showed compassion for the 267 strangers standing nearest to the nail-spewing bombs. They wove goodness into the memory of the Marathon bombing.

But there was a problem, and only the White House could solve it.

The One Fund was too unconventional for the IRS. We had applied for 501(c)(3) status under the tax law so contributors could claim a deduction. The IRS would permit that—*if* the beneficiaries, the shattered victims filling Boston's hospitals, demonstrated their "need" by producing hospital bills, tax returns, and the like. We countered that the One Fund was distributing gifts, not paying patients' bills. Donors contributed to the fund without conditions, and the fund would give out money without conditions. If it went to pay hospital bills, fine. If it was used to take the kids to Disney World, also fine. The law, the IRS lawyers said, was the law.

President Obama and Vice President Biden called several times to say if there was anything they could do to help Boston, just ask. I asked. If the IRS denied deductions to One Fund donors, I explained to Joe Biden, that would discourage giving and limit the payout to people who had lost eyes, legs, and children. The IRS, I added, had enough trouble with the Republicans attacking it for investigating conservative groups. It would be a shame if someone leaked the news that IRS bureaucrats were blocking help to the victims of the deadliest terrorist bombing since 9/11 . . .

The problem went away. The One Fund made new tax law.

But that was not clear yet a week after the bombing when I met with big donors and told them they might not be able to write off their contributions. Not one executive blinked. I expected no less from the Boston business community, which in my twenty years in office never let the city down.

Cooperation among the different tiers of government—city, state, federal—was unprecedented. The White House responded to all our requests. And Governor Patrick and I agreed in minutes on who should do what, and backed each other up in public statements. The tone we set was communicated down the chain of command, where city cops and state troopers shared information and worked in tandem on the criminal investigation.

"From the very beginning, the senior people on the scene or arriving at the scene felt the need to find one another," according to a Harvard study of emergency management after the bombing. "They realized that the situation needed them to come together." On the day of the bombing, that saved lives. ("Every person who left the scene alive is alive today.") The teamwork was rehearsed. Years before 9/11, I sent my department heads to Virginia for briefings on emergency preparedness. Since 9/11 we had drilled, exercised, played out in real time how to respond to attacks on big public events like the Democratic Convention in 2004 and the annual July Fourth celebration on the Esplanade. "Boston Strong was not a chance result," the Harvard researchers concluded. "It was, instead, the product of years of investment of time and hard work by people across multiple jurisdictions, levels of government, agencies and organizations."

About the FBI, the lead agency in the hunt for the bombers, my feelings are mixed. On the one hand, the agents were committed to getting the bad guys. On the other, the bureau's caution seemed motivated by fear of making a mistake.

By late Wednesday, Ed Davis and I were losing patience. Security cameras at stores along Boylston Street, including Lord & Taylor across from the second bomb blast, had recorded the bombers' images, but the bureau was resisting pressure to release the pictures. The feds did not want the suspects to know they had been caught on tape. Apparently, some agents thought the two young men (it was not yet known they were brothers) might show up around the Cathedral of the Holy Cross on Thursday morning, drawn by President Obama, who'd be speaking at an interfaith service. I hoped that risky plan wasn't the only reason the FBI was reluctant to share the tapes with the earth's population.

Like Ed Davis, I was disturbed to discover that, long before the bombing, the FBI had not shared with state and local police its intel about Tamerlan Tsarnaev's mysterious 2012 trip to Dagestan, a Russian republic. According to a 2014 report by the House Committee on Homeland Security, "even in the days after the attack as the manhunt was ongoing," the FBI did not inform Davis of its Tsarnaev investigation. The FBI and the CIA had hoarded information that, if shared, might have prevented 9/11. The Homeland Security Committee report identified four "systemic weaknesses" in federal counterterrorism efforts prior to the bombing. The first weakness—"insufficient cooperation and information sharing between Federal agencies and local law enforcement"—suggests that 9/11 had not been enough to shake up the FBI's insular culture.*

I decided to notch up the pressure to release the videos. In an interview with CNN's John King, a Dorchester boy, I surfaced the Lord & Taylor intelligence. So that cat was out of the bag. Reddit was displaying an image said to be taken from a security camera that fit the bomber's rumored description—white baseball cap, dark backpack. Only it wasn't the bomber but a young man who worked in my office! The FBI warned the media of the "unintended consequences" of running such images.

Lynching was one of them. The cover of Thursday's *New York Post* raised that danger. Under the headline "Bag Men" and flanked by the line "Feds Seek These Two Pictured at Boston Marathon" was a photograph of two innocent Massachusetts men, sixteen-year-old Salaheddin Barhoum and twenty-four-year-old Yassine Zaimi, seen talking near the finish line. The *Post* cover story put their lives at risk. Before the worst happened, the FBI had to release the video of

* "The FBI has repeatedly asserted that even knowing what it now knows, it would not have revisited the Tsarnaev investigation. This case-closed mindset cannot keep pace with the evolving threat of terrorism here at home." See "How Did Tsarnaev Go Off FBI Radar?" by Representative Michael McCaul, Republican of Texas, chairman of the House Committee on Homeland Security, and Representative Bill Keating, Democrat of Massachusetts, a senior member of the committee, *Boston Globe,* March 27, 2014.

the real bombers. I silently vowed to appeal to the president if the bureau didn't budge.

On Thursday afternoon, it budged.

That morning, passing bomb-sniffing dogs patrolling the streets, I arrived at the cathedral before the president. Sitting alone in a basement room, I had time to think. I sensed the public mood falling. Alarmed that the bombers were still at large, people were losing confidence in the investigation. They were also shaken (I know I was) by graphic media accounts of amputations. I wanted to do something—anything—to raise morale, even if only for a news cycle. But what?

I don't obsess about comments in the media. Usually. But a statement to a reporter from a local professor had stuck in my craw. Referring to my retirement at the end of 2013, he said, "It is unfortunate that one of the last impressions people will have of his mayoralty is him in a wheelchair, almost sidelined at a time of crisis." The phrase "in a wheelchair" got to me. Hadn't FDR led the country through depression and war in a wheelchair?

At the interfaith service a succession of speakers mounted the pulpit to address the audience. A separate microphone, adjusted to the height of my wheelchair, was set up for me. When it was my turn to speak, my son whispered to me, "Dad, I'll wheel you over to the microphone." Suddenly, I knew what to do. "Tommy," I said, "I'm the mayor. Wheel me to the pulpit. I'm going to stand up."

If you watched the service, you saw the struggle I had doing it. I could feel the president and Mrs. Obama and the two thousand people in the cathedral rooting for me. With Tommy tipping the wheelchair forward, I put my hands on the arms and pushed. It was no good. I tucked my elbows further back and pushed harder. Bit-ing my lower lip against a twinge of pain, grabbing the lectern for balance, I stood up. The enclosed pulpit hid the line connecting my catheter to the bag on the wheelchair.

"Good morning," I said, as the sun lit the stained-glass windows. "And it is a good morning because we are together. We are one Boston. No adversity, no challenge, nothing can tear down the resilience in the heart of this city and its people. . . . I have never loved it . . . more than I do today." I described the acts of caring that unfolded within seconds of the bombing, and then I remembered the dead: "We say goodbye to the young boy with the big heart, Martin Richard, . . . we'll miss Krystle Campbell and celebrate her spirit that brought her to the Marathon year after year . . . and we mourn Lu Lingzi, who came to the city in search of education, and found new friends."

Boston's worst moment, I said, was the beginning of Boston's finest hour: "Even with the smell of smoke in the air, and blood on the streets, and with tears in our eyes, we triumphed over that hateful act on Monday afternoon. . . . Because this is Boston, a city with courage, compassion, and strength that knows no bounds."

Governor Patrick followed, moving me when he said, "Mayor Menino started Monday morning frustrated he couldn't be at the finish line this time as he always is. And then late that afternoon, checked himself out of the hospital to help this city, our city, face down this tragedy." His last line—"We will rise, and we will endure"—picked up on my gesture. Reporters are suckers for symbols. A *Los Angeles Times* headline was typical: "Mayor Menino: Symbol of a Resilient Boston." The story described the reaction to my speech—"He pulled himself from his wheelchair to the loudest applause of the day"—and noted that "in some ways, the mayor has become a potent symbol as a wounded Boston tries to heal."

It quoted one young woman visiting the makeshift Copley Square memorial to the bombing victims, and, boy, did she get my message! "He can't even walk and he's here to comfort all of us," she said. "It shows how strong our leaders are here — how strong the people are — that if anything were to happen . . . [we'd] drop what [we're] doing and . . . take care of each other." People still tell me that speech lifted their spirits.

On Friday morning I reversed the stand I had staked out on Monday afternoon: Terror must not be allowed to disrupt daily life. Boston had nothing to fear.

Boston had plenty to fear that Friday morning. The release of the store security videos panicked the bombers, the Tsarnaev brothers, into running. They didn't get far, about a mile from their Cambridge home, when they stopped to ambush a twenty-six-year-old MIT policeman, Sean A. Collier. In a bungled attempt to steal his gun, they snuck up behind his patrol car and shot him five times. Crossing the Charles River into Boston, they carjacked a Mercedes SUV in Allston. The older brother, Tamerlan, waved a silver pistol at the driver and said, "I just killed a policeman in Cambridge." And for nearly ninety minutes, the brothers made him, a young Chinese immigrant-entrepreneur named Danny, drive from one ATM to another emptying his bank account. When they stopped for gas back on the Cambridge side of the Charles, Danny bolted and alerted police.

In the SUV, the brothers led cruisers on a chase that ended in the early hours of Friday in Watertown, near the Boston line, in a shootout that left one officer, Richard H. Donohue Jr., critically wounded. Tamerlan was killed. Dzhokhar, the younger brother, escaped. After searching for him till dawn, police thought he might have got away.

He was a dangerous kid. In the Watertown gunfight, the brothers threw pipe bombs at police.

Dzhokhar Tsarnaev wasn't all Boston had to fear that morning. There were reports of a man carrying a suspicious package near the federal courthouse in the Seaport District, of another suspicious package in a cab at Charlesgate, of pipe bombs buried in Kenmore Square, of a dangerous character on an Amtrak train . . . Governor Patrick ticked them off in a six A.M. call. Monday's question was Friday's: How big could this get?

The security people recommended a lockdown of Boston and municipalities bordering it. Not a state of emergency, Patrick said. A million people would be asked, not ordered, to "shelter-in-place."

On Monday I vowed, "We will not let terror take us over." The reports streaming in on Friday morning—earlier in the week we had refused to be panicked by such rumors. I doubted the brothers had confederates. I still believed they acted alone.

Danny, the owner of the carjacked SUV, said they discussed driving to New York to bomb Times Square. Suppose Dzhokhar was still in Watertown. Only one measure could prevent him from seizing another car and carrying out their plan: stopping all travel so any moving civilian vehicle would stand out. That was my reason for going along with shelter-in-place.

"Do it," I said.

"There is a massive manhunt under way," the governor announced at a press conference. "To assist that . . . we're asking people to shelter-in-place, in other words to stay indoors with the doors locked and do not open the doors to anyone other than a properly identified law enforcement officer, and that applies here in Watertown where we are right now, [but] also in Cambridge . . . and at this point, all of Boston. All of Boston."

Without detailing them, Police Commissioner Ed Davis, speaking next, emphasized the reports that justified the lockdown: "Within the last half hour we have received information that I have communicated to Mayor Menino. . . . Mayor Menino asked me to come here and to tell you . . . that the shelter-in-place recommendation has been extended throughout the City of Boston."

Shelter-in-place was an overreaction. That was clear Friday evening, when, minutes after the governor called it off, Dzhokhar Tsarnaev was found. After being confined to his house all day, David Henneberry, who lived on Franklin Street in Watertown, less than a mile from where Tsarnaev ditched the SUV, went outside to get some fresh air. He noticed two paint rollers on his lawn. He figured they had fallen from the cover on his boat. When he'd wrapped the *Slip Away II* in white plastic in the fall, he'd put paint rollers under the bottom edge of the wrap to protect the surface of the boat. He climbed a stepladder, peeled back the cover, and looked inside.

Minutes later an officer's voice came over the police scanner: "We're getting a report from Watertown of 67 Franklin Street. They have a boat with blood in it. . . . I've got the owner of the house here. He says there's a body in the boat." Absent shelter-in-place, Henneberry might have discovered Dzhokhar Tsarnaev earlier.

I was in Watertown with my team in the city SUV when Commissioner Davis walked over, leaned his head into the vehicle, and said, "We got him." Dot Joyce's tweet—"We got him, we got him. Thank God, the search is over"—was the first the world heard of it.

The scanner came alive with chatter. I picked up a microphone. To the hundreds of officers who had worked around the clock for five days to bring the bombers to justice, I said: "People of Boston are proud of you. Especially the mayor of Boston. I'm very proud of what you've done." Silence. Then the scanner crackled and a voice said something I won't forget: "We did it for you, boss."

That night thousands poured into the streets to cheer convoys of police vehicles. When I returned to the Parkman House, the city-owned townhouse on Beacon Hill where I was staying since leaving the hospital, a crowd of young people were celebrating on the Common. I rolled down the window. They were singing "God Bless America."

Ed Davis called. "The kids are celebrating in the Fenway," he said. Should the police begin to shut it down? "Let 'em blow off steam," I said. "They've been sheltered-in-place for twelve hours. They deserve to whoop it up."

Governor Patrick and I were both retiring at the end of our terms. Our timing was perfect. If we had run for reelection, the lockdown would have been used against us. Attack ads would have depicted Boston as a scene from *Planet of the Apes:* the "eerily empty" downtown streets, the traffic-less highways, the shuttered train yards, the closed businesses, universities, and courthouses, the locked City Hall and State House. The ads would contrast what I said all week with what I said to George Stephanopoulos on ABC's *This Week* two days after Dzhokhar's capture:

ME: These terrorists want[ed] to . . . hold the city hostage and stop the economy. . . . Look at what happened on Friday. The whole city was on lockdown, no businesses open, nobody leaving their homes. . . .

GEORGE: Well, let me ask you about that lockdown. Because some have suggested that it was an overreaction to lock down the city—that it was actually giving the terrorists exactly what they wanted.

George spoke my Monday lines to indict my Friday decision.

Yet if shelter-in-place was a miscalculation by elected officials, it was a triumph for citizens. "We asked," Governor Patrick said a year after the bombing. "Frankly, it was an amazing thing . . . that people . . . complied."

Not everyone saw it that way. "The Boston bombing provided the opportunity for the government to turn what should have been a police investigation into a military-style occupation of an American city," Ron Paul argued. A military-style occupation? "There has been no law mentioned," a police official said, "or any idea that if you go outside [you'll] be arrested." People stayed home voluntarily.

Paul again: "This unprecedented act should frighten us as much or more than the attack itself." Really? Should it "frighten us" that to contain a common threat, citizens did what their government requested? That by depriving terrorists of the option of hiding in the crowd, they took responsibility for public safety? That Bostonians consented to limit their individual freedom in order to preserve their civic liberty? This unprecedented act should make us curious why, for thirteen hours on a fine April day, 650,000 Boston residents put community before self, and how their city came to inspire their loyalty. Trust in government is at an all-time low. Perhaps the Boston story holds lessons on how to regain it.

After five terms as mayor, I left office with an 80 percent approval rating. That is not a tribute to me but to a style of governing that bridges the gap between the citizen and the city. I paid attention to the fundamentals of urban life—clean streets, public safety, good schools, neighborhood commerce. I listened to what people said they wanted from government. Call my City Hall and you never got an answering machine. People trusted government because it heard them. Because they could talk to it. Because it kept its word. And because it was credible about things people could see, they accepted its judgment on important things they couldn't. In an "amazing" show of self-government, all of Boston acted as one on April 19, 2013. This book tries to explain why, as I told George Stephanopoulos, "Boston did a great job that day."

Chapter 1

From Hyde Park to City Hall

I want the city of Boston to be for everybody what Hyde Park was for me.

— *from my first inaugural address, 1994*

I GREW UP in a good world. Neighborhoods were safe. Union jobs were plentiful. Parents fought but rarely split. There was a basic security to life. It wasn't like that everywhere in the 1950s, not by a long shot. But it was like that for me coming of age in Hyde Park.

I was a progressive mayor. In the country's youngest city (by age), I embraced the innovation economy. I celebrated Boston's mix of peoples and cultures. I championed gay rights. According to a gay community newspaper, there were so many gay men in my first administration that "you couldn't swing a dead cat without hitting one." The title of this book, *Mayor for a New America*, is accurate. But my public values look back to an Old America. To schools that prepared young people for jobs. To a secure and growing middle class. To stable communities, close neighborhoods, and strong families.

Franklin D. Roosevelt, raised in Hyde Park on Hudson, was once asked what he wanted for Americans. "What I had growing up," he said. "Good health, security, the leisure to read and travel and develop my interests. And I want that for everybody." That's how I felt about *my* Hyde Park legacy — the good life people can have living in Boston's neighborhoods. And I wanted that for everybody.

Hyde Park, annexed in 1912, was the last addition to Boston. After Hyde Park the city was complete.

Hyde Park fills Boston's southernmost corner. But partly because you can drive from downtown to the New Hampshire border quicker than to parts of Hyde Park, to many Bostonians it might as well be Mars.

Boston pols included. To them Hyde Park was the sticks. They had no idea it was so vote-rich until I made it my base to run for mayor. What one columnist called "the eight-hundred pound gorilla of Hyde Park politics" was loose, and it was too late to stop him.

Until the 1970s, Hyde Park was a center of heavy industry. There was a Westinghouse plant, an Allis-Chalmers factory, and, to service these giants, small foundries and metalworking shops spread all over.

My father, a member of the Machinists Union, worked at Westinghouse. Lots of men in our "lunch pail neighborhood" worked there. I could mess up in school, I thought, and still land a job at the plant.

I did work there the summer of my senior year in high school. By then my dad was a foreman. I noticed how he heard the men out. It was his way of showing respect. That was my first lesson in politics.

I'm a bad talker ("Mumbles Menino") but a good listener. I won ten elections. Maybe a politician who stops talking long enough to listen is a breath of fresh air to voters.

> I am your mayor. You came here seeking a better life just like my grandparents.
>
> — *addressing Boston's newest immigrants in my 1994 inaugural*

As a child I learned about the problems facing newcomers to America — the same problems with visas, language, housing, the bureaucracy, and the schools facing Boston's immigrants from Latin America, Asia, and Africa today. In my first inaugural, to these new Americans of thirty-four nationalities I said: "I am your mayor. . . . If you have arrived in Boston, like my grandmother, speaking no English, I will make sure you get the help you need to learn the language. Here and now, I tell you, I will institute a full range of English-as-a-second-language programs."

To help these folks navigate city government, I established the Office of New Bostonians in City Hall. It connects newcomers to city services with few questions asked. Immigrants are welcome in Boston regardless of their "status."

So when immigrants' rights groups revealed that, under an innocent-sounding program begun after 9/11, my police were forwarding information to federal officials that got moms and dads deported, I hit the roof. The police had better things to do with their time. I did not become mayor to throw hardworking people out of the country.

My mother, Susan, was a Mother Teresa to new immigrants in Hyde Park, starting at home. We occupied the first floor of a two-family house on Hyde Park Avenue. My aunt lived on the second floor along with my grandparents. My grandfather Thomas Menino was from Grottaminarda, a village in Avellino in the Campania region of southern Italy, the area known as the *Mezzogiorno,* which means "midday" and refers to the strength of the noon sun. Its inhabitants called it *La Miseria* for the privations that filled the ships to America. My cousin painted a mural of my grandfather showing him sitting in Grottaminarda with his suitcase, waiting for a ship to cross the ocean that occupies most of the painting. His destination is an American city marked by its skyline. In the mural, so big it filled a wall in my outer office at City Hall, he looks sad but determined. Attracted by the opportunity it offered to practice his trade—laborer—he settled in Hyde Park, his American Dream before it was mine.

Next door to our house my grandfather bought a six-decker for family members still in Italy. Each group stayed a few years, working seven days a week and eating a diet of pasta to scrape together a down payment for a house. Then they moved out and a new group moved in. My mother, who spoke fluent Italian, helped them fill out job applications, pay their bills, and enroll their children in the schools. She guided them at every stage of their journey to American citizenship. Eventually she extended her hand from family to strangers, and from Italians to immigrants from Greece, Ireland, and other countries.

I was twenty-one when she died with my six-year-old brother, David, in her arms. She'd had a hole in her heart. My father wouldn't leave the house for weeks. His grief was total, like his love.

Carl Menino was a remarkable guy. On Sundays and on special occasions he wore only the best, down to his silk shorts and cashmere socks. I owe my taste in fine clothes to him. People expect public officials to dress well, and I tried not to disappoint. Three or four times a week, drawn by the discounts on goods that had not sold at the specialty stores in New York and Boston, I'd drop by Filene's Basement on Washington Street. Its closing, in 2009, was a blow to my wallet.

My father was also a semi-pro baseball player. Second baseman on a team that traveled all over New England. After he was spiked turning a double play, he thought, *What am I doing still playing ball? I've got a wife and kids to support,* and hung up his cleats. Carl worked thirty-five years at the same plant. During the Second World War it ran three shifts making propellers and anchors for battleships and carriers. In the 50s it produced giant fans for highway tunnels. On the site today is the Academy of the Pacific Rim, a multicultural charter high school for students from some of the countries that put the Westinghouse Fan Division out of business.

While Carl was mostly good-natured, if the Red Sox lost you couldn't talk to him. (Which in that era meant a lot of silences.) And he was stubborn. In 1956 he went to Eliot Ford in Jackson Square to buy a new car, arriving at eight in the morning and staying till five. He had a figure in mind and wouldn't budge. Outlasting the salesman, he got the car for his price.

Carl took night school classes at Northeastern to improve himself, and he pushed me to continue my education. He sent me to a parochial high school, but I coasted. I'd go to the library with my friends and we'd work for a while; then we'd close the books and hang out at Friendly's Ice Cream in Dedham. "[Tom] used to say, when I got after him to go to college, 'Truman never went to college,'" Carl said in a 1983 interview. "He must have told me that 1,000 times."

Harry Truman: my political hero. I hung his portrait behind my desk at City Hall. A plainspoken man of the people. It was only when I read David McCullough's biography that I learned Harry was also a scholar of Greek and Roman history. The public library was his college.

Carl was thrilled by my election to the City Council. He was nervous I wouldn't win and marched up and down the streets of

Hyde Park, knocking on every door and asking everybody he knew to vote for me. It was a lesson I carried with me for the rest of my political career — never take any person or vote for granted. A decade later, when I was elected mayor, he wasn't around. He did see me graduate from the University of Massachusetts Boston in 1988 — at forty-five — a proud day in both our lives.

My parents lived their values. My mother modeled service to others. If I hadn't gone into politics, following her example I probably would have been a social worker. She was the strongest influence on my life. My father, a Westinghouse lifer, modeled loyalty and hard work. By always respecting the dignity of my challenged brother, they showed me the meaning of equality.

Beyond my family, another figure looming over my youth was "the Deacon," the tall Irish cop who walked the beat in our neighborhood. Kids cursed his timing — he'd show up just when the fun was starting. And I squirmed when he'd stop by the house to say hello to my parents. Still, he made you feel that the government of the city was your friend. As mayor I promised to restore this "symbol of welcome and security," to bring back the "cop on the beat on foot in your neighborhood . . . to make you and your children feel safe again." Chapter 3 details how I tried to make that promise a reality.

From preschool to high school I hung out, played ball, and went to the movies with the same group of guys. My oldest friends, they remained my best friends. I was the shyest of the bunch. The idea of me telling a joke *was* a joke. I could hit a baseball. I was tough on the basketball court. That won me some respect. If I spoke of doing anything when I grew up, it was being an engineer. A bridge builder. But a politician? Not in this life. As I put it in a 1993 interview, "I was always involved in the cancer fund, the heart fund, helping raise money. But for me to run for office? That shocked people because I was never an out-front guy. Never."

I had twelve years of nuns who used to use their sticks on me.
—*from my "Nuns' Story"*

I'm reluctant to say much about school. Because my teeth and lips would not cooperate, I talked out of the side of my mouth, mumbling decades before I was called "Mumbles." I had trouble enunciating (a nun ordered me to mime the words because my singing was wrecking the school choir), and dreaded being called on in class. Mostly I sat in silence and fidgeted. The nuns encouraged kids who didn't need encouragement, not those who did. Me, I got the stick. One time I spilled a bottle of ink over some brand-new textbooks. A nun charged down the aisle of desks with a stick about a yard long, backpedaled for maximum hitting power, and whaled me. "Sister, it's washable ink!" I protested, but she kept whaling.

I can think of one way my unhappy experience of school shaped my school policies as a public official. Besides giving awards for top grades, I handed out special awards first to kids in my council district then to the graduating classes of every school in Boston. It became a twenty-nine-year tradition. In six award ceremonies, two a night, I put the spotlight on kids who'd never won anything before. Kids who tutored classmates during lunchtime. Older kids who stuck up for younger ones being bullied. Kids who smiled through tough times. Special-needs kids, kids who struggled with English (I could sympathize), kids who worked hard because school came hard. School Spirit Awards, we called them. The students got a kick out of it, dressing up for the occasion—girls in fancy dresses, boys in suits (sometimes with the tags still on!). Their parents often thanked us with tears in their eyes. My last years in office we were giving awards to kids whose parents had won before them. And some of those parents had become teachers.

It's time the schools recognized moral qualities like compassion and persistence and not just natural gifts like intelligence. If I could wave a magic wand, teachers would honor not just being first but being kind, not just grades but effort, not just brains but character.

> This is the choice, then, in 1960. Shall we go forward? Shall we move with the times? . . . I believe we must go forward. You have to decide what to think. Are you satisfied with things as they are? . . . The campaign is now over. The responsibility has ceased to be ours who are candidates, and it is now yours, the citizens of this great Republic. . . . You must make your judgment between sitting and moving.
>
> —*Senator John F. Kennedy, from the last speech of the 1960 presidential campaign, at Faneuil Hall on the night of November 7, election eve*

My parents didn't pay much attention to politics, and I followed their lead. But in 1960 you couldn't live in Massachusetts and be Catholic and ignore politics. Not with Senator John F. Kennedy running for the Democratic nomination in the spring and the White House in the fall. My career in politics began on election eve, when I cut a night school class to catch JFK's wind-up speech at Faneuil Hall.

I took literally Kennedy's stirring call to get America moving. I was in the crowd outside when he came down the Hall's thirteen granite steps. He had one last stop to make: a rally at nearby Boston Garden. As his limousine pulled away, I began to run after it. And as it sped up, I ran faster, chasing JFK through the cobblestone streets of old Boston toward the Garden, bright as day in the floodlit night. I'd always avoided drawing attention to myself, yet here I was shouting "JFK! JFK!" and waving my arms like a madman while running for all I was worth. In the miniseries based on this book, Tom Cruise should have no trouble covering the distance in one take.

My start in politics came six months later.

Hollywood would quickly pass over my work history. I spent one summer as a laborer at Bird & Sons in a suburban mill town. I had to force my beefy body through a two-by-two opening into steam-generating furnaces and scrub them until they were clean and I was filthy. When I got home at night, my mother wouldn't let me into the house until I changed my clothes.

I also worked at a Mattapan eatery, Simco's on the Bridge, taking orders for the famous foot-long hot dogs. After my shift, which ran from three in the afternoon to two in the morning, I'd drive down Blue Hill Avenue for a sandwich at the G&G Delicatessen, a landmark of a long-gone Jewish neighborhood. In the intervening decades, as restaurants shuttered and stores went out of business, the once-lively avenue became a boulevard of broken dreams. My first commitment as mayor was to restore its commercial hub, Grove Hall, to something like its old vitality. I didn't drink coffee, but I was a regular at the local Dunkin' Donuts, my first stop on the way to City Hall. Greeting customers, I'd feel for the pulse of neighborhood recovery. By my last term, Dunkin' Donuts was one store in a bustling shopping mall development, and from planters on the median strip, flowers bloomed on Blue Hill Avenue.

What possessed Metropolitan Life to hire me as a salesman? Affirmative action? Arrogance — a belief that there was *no one* they couldn't train to sell? Or was it that I was a big young guy with dark wavy hair who looked presentable in a suit and tie? Whatever it was, I'm grateful. Because I had met Angela, and I couldn't ask her to marry a guy with no prospects.

She was playing on the Hyde Park tennis court next to mine. Somehow her ball kept veering off course and into my end of the court. She'd trot over, apologize for interrupting my game, and trot back.

She didn't need to apologize.

We clicked. We went to the West Roxbury drive-in, shared sodas at the drugstore in Roslindale Square, took walks in the Turtle Pond Reservation in Hyde Park. "And when it came to dancing back when we were dating," Angela told the *Boston Herald* columnist Joe Fitzgerald, "if I could drag him onto the floor just once, that would be it for the night." She was pretty, bright, funny, and compassionate. A Roslindale girl, but you can't have everything. I've often been asked if becoming acting mayor of Boston wasn't the luckiest break of my life. No, I reply.

He was exactly what I was looking for.

—Joe Timilty, in a 2009 interview

Summer 1961. Kelly Field in Hyde Park. Boston Park League baseball under the lights. I'm there to watch friends play for the Bottomly Braves. One of the Braves, Mike Donato, a Boston College High star, introduces me to a young candidate for the Boston City Council, Joe Timilty, an ex-marine whose uncle was a Boston police commissioner in the 1930s.

Close-up on me. This is a big moment in my life.

My dad hated politics. But one day he asked me to hand out flyers for his friend Charlie Patrone, a state rep. That was my entire background in politics. Joe didn't care. He needed volunteers for his first campaign. Forty-eight years later he told *Boston Magazine,* "He worked at it." That sounds like me.

Joe won his seat on the council. And I joined his organization. Every campaign season we'd come together to reelect Joe. Me, I soldiered on at Met Life.

I was the world's worst salesman. I couldn't talk people into deals that sounded good but tripled their premiums. I didn't believe my own pitch. How could I expect them to?

Met Life would carry a bum salesman. But not one who helped organize a union. I thought I was a big shot sitting across the table from management, but I was a target. They found a pretext to fire me.

I was twenty-six, with a new baby, no degree, and no job.

I turned to Joe for help. He got me "on" the Boston Redevelopment Authority (BRA).

My job was to move small businesses out of the way of a federal highway slicing through Boston. Protest politics stopped the highway, but not before bulldozers had scraped all signs of life off once-thriving commercial arteries from Roxbury to Charlestown. The "Inner Belt" was the dying gasp of Boston's "urban removal" era. My vision of government was born then. It was the opposite of everything happening around me. Government should be about helping people, not destroying their way of life, which is how merchants in its path saw the federal bulldozer.

I think of an old-timer who ran a hardware store in Charlestown. Waving a slick brochure that made "relocation" sound like a day at Revere Beach, I approached him as he stood behind his counter. He pointed a gun at me and told me to get out of his store.

Two wrestlers writhing in a muddy pit.

— the Boston Globe, *commenting on the 1975 mayoral campaign between Kevin White and Joe Timilty*

Long before I ran for mayor, politics was my profession. Besides working next to Joe Timilty in his campaigns, I helped run Jimmy Carter's field organization in Pennsylvania in 1976 and 1980. I took to politics. Especially the inside game — planning the events, deploying the forces, and getting the forces and the candidate to the events on time . . . a list as long as your arm.

I took to the details. In office, I earned the nickname "Mayor Pothole" for photographing potholes, broken streetlights, and abandoned cars in my travels around the city and sending the pictures to the relevant departments and then following up. Campaigns are full of potholes. A fellow who keeps track of them is good to have around.

I was Joe's "body man." I saw him the first thing in the morning and the last thing at night. Messages to Joe went through me. Tell me something with the bark off, that's how he heard it. I had no agenda of my own. I gave your message level.

I was paid peanuts for my work. I would have paid to do it. My peers trusted me. I saw my merit in their eyes.

I stored that good feeling against the bad moments.

There are lots of those in campaigns. The candidate unloads on you and you've got to take it. Or pretends you didn't tell him something when you did. And the person who asked you to tell him that something? From then on, he's your enemy. Or the candidate is indiscreet about another member of the team, and you can't look at him again without being reminded of what you shouldn't know. I make the candidate sound petty. I've been the candidate. I'm partly talking about myself. You say things you regret. It's the tension.

The strain of performing. The self-criticism. The self-pity. Imagine working for LBJ. Now imagine being LBJ.

Joe's fights against Kevin White were epic battles. Three times we took the field, and three times we lost.

He was an incumbent. They win every time in Boston. (I should know.) Why did we think we had a chance?

Because the voters resented Kevin's using them as a springboard to higher office. Kevin White was first elected in November 1967. He ran for governor in 1970, losing in a landslide. George McGovern asked him to be his running mate in 1972. Ted Kennedy vetoed that — he wouldn't share the national stage with another Irish Catholic from Massachusetts. But the feeler stimulated Kevin's ambition. He was preparing to run for president in 1976 when Boston's busing crisis derailed his plans.

I was the opposite of Kevin White. I wanted to be mayor of Boston. Period. That was my pact with the people. They were staying put in the city; so was I. In my first race, I pledged to serve only two terms. Later, I made that two terms a century.

Knowing I wasn't going anywhere kept city employees and contractors on their toes. And having no designs on their jobs smoothed my relations with a string of Republican governors from Bill Weld to Mitt Romney. Weld and company knew that helping Boston would not hurt them. By contrast, Mayor Ray Flynn's noises about challenging Weld invited the governor to ignore the city.

We also thought White was beatable because of the "climate of corruption" in his administration, an issue we stoked in our slogan "Joe Timilty, Honestly." Kevin's fundraising techniques included forced contributions from contractors and city employees, who paid in cash at a suite at the Parker House. We threw this and more at him in 1975. His camp replied in kind. Days before the election, Kevin's police commissioner charged that the Mob was behind Joe. The *Herald* called the campaign "a nasty, negative free-for-all." Kevin barely hung on, winning by 4.8 percent.

I was the big loser in the election. My work for Joe went for nothing. And Kevin White fired me from the BRA. I didn't blame him. I would have done the same thing.

It was a deliverance. I would have stayed in that rut until retirement. That's how I see the firing now. I was ashamed then.

For the second time in our marriage, I was jobless. Angela didn't reproach me for sinking my life into Joe's career. *I* reproached me. I was getting nothing out of politics. I was going nowhere in *my* career.

For the second time, Joe bailed me out. A state senator by then, he got me a staff job on one of his committees.

During my time at the State House, I stayed in touch with the city through someone I met on Joe's campaign. Often identified as "a longtime counselor to the Kennedys," Gerry Doherty was an old pro from Charlestown. He became my friend and mentor, inviting me to join the Park Street Corporation, a discussion group on urban issues led by a Paulist priest, Robert Quinn. I showed up for every meeting, and learned a lot from the academics, high-tech entrepreneurs, and developers who spoke.

I was the guy who supplied the bagels. But Gerry saw something in me. "Most of the people you meet, they flash their teeth and shake your hand, while at the same time they're looking over your shoulder," he told the journalist Joe Keohane. "He didn't do that. When he walked into a room, he wouldn't galvanize it, but by the end of the night he could tell you exactly who was there, what they did, what they didn't do."

In the post-Watergate era, when nobody trusted politicians, Gerry thought my "quietness of style" might come across as sincerity (it was) and help make me a successful candidate. I agreed. But for what office?

The Boston City Council? Its nine members ran "at-large." I couldn't win a citywide race. All my connections were in Hyde Park. In 1982 the playing field shifted my way. The council was expanded to four at-large and nine district seats. District 5 covered Hyde Park and slivers of other neighborhoods, including Roslindale and West Roxbury. The legislature had to approve the change. Joe Timilty looked out for my interests at the State House. The Hyde Park seat? "It was created for him," he said.

Just as I started up the political ladder, Joe stepped off it. Following his third defeat by Kevin White, in 1979, he soured on politics and resigned his Senate seat five years later. He moved his growing family out of their small Mattapan ranch to a more spacious house in a suburb of Boston. After 1984, the *Globe* reported, Joe engaged in "an intense pursuit of money, losing many of his old contacts and friends." His new friends were "big-money developers." I believe he made some bad decisions. In May 1993, after a trial in U.S. District Court, Joe was convicted of being part of a "conspiracy to commit fraud." I was mayor when he was sentenced to four months in federal prison. The contrast in our fortunes was painful to me. And tragic for Joe, a guy who poured his heart into helping those who had no voice. One of his greatest legacies was founding Camp Joy, an oasis for kids with special needs.

When is the last time a city councilor fried anybody?

—*speaking at a Cleary Square debate in 1983*

I was a campaign operative. An organizer. "An extension of Timilty." A backstage guy whose career nearly ended the second he stepped on stage.

I announced my candidacy for City Council in the backyard of my childhood home at 1449 Hyde Park Avenue. I got through that fine. Not so the first candidates' forum held at the Knights of Columbus Hall in Hyde Park. Before the debate started, the candidates were scheduled to introduce themselves and say why we were running. All I had to do was read a three-sentence statement. All? No one liable to use "condoms" for "condos" would say "all."

When we drove up, I said I couldn't do it. Those were my friends inside! It would be using them to ask for their votes.

My campaign staff, sacrificing their time and energy to put me over, threatened bodily harm. I relented.

I can still see that lectern. The microphone. The crowd.

Standing in the wings, I took a deep breath, then walked out on the stage.

And froze.

I was supposed to begin "I just want you to know I'm running for . . . ," but managed only "Ah . . . ," then nothing. Today that moment would have gone viral on the Web. Mercifully, there were no cameras in the hall.

For what felt like a week, I stood mute at the lectern. Finally, when the crowd was about out of patience, my friend Peggy Gannon tiptoed on stage and tugged the sleeve of my jacket. It broke the trance.

I spoke.

They cheered. Not for what I said but for saying anything. I didn't care. It felt great.

On a hot Fourth of July I knew I would win.

Angela and I had spent the day climbing hilly streets and walking up front steps to drop off leaflets. Late in the afternoon, wiping the sweat off my glasses, I saw my leading opponent drive by, windows closed, in his air-conditioned car. "Let's go to dinner," I said to Angela. "This thing is over."

The campaign had its moments.

There were six candidates. To break out of the pack, one said he'd give $30,000 of his $32,000 salary to local charities. "How is the gentleman going to live?" I asked in a Cleary Square debate. "It sounds to me like this is not going to be his full-time job. I'll be a full-time councilor!" Not taking that cheap shot would have been political malpractice.

Another candidate, a retired state police lieutenant, ran on the death penalty. Nothing but death. "Menino, Timilty's lackey, is against the death penalty," he declared at one forum. I'd had it with death. I got to my feet. "This is a campaign for City Council," I said in a sarcastic voice. "When is the last time a city councilor fried anybody? Talk about the real issues."

The race drew the attention of the local PBS station, WGBH, which followed me along the campaign trail for weeks. They made a half-hour documentary. I'm not sure if it won any awards but it was definitely a glimpse into neighborhood politics done what some have termed "the Menino way," one door, one vote at a time.

In 1983 the only issue was the state of Boston's neighborhoods. Kevin White, in charge at City Hall since 1968, was the "downtown mayor." He boasted that Boston was a "world-class city" of skyscrapers, tourist hotels, and harborside concerts. The neighborhoods felt left behind.

Mayoral candidates identified with White lost in the primary. The two finalists attacked "the downtown interests" and, to my ear, sounded not just pro-neighborhood but anti-development, even anti-business. After sixteen years of Kevin White, "development" versus "the neighborhoods" was good politics, but was it good policy? As city councilor, I promised to bring development *to* the neighborhoods by reviving fading commercial districts, beginning with Roslindale Square, a comeback story told in Chapter 4.

The district had my name on it. I carried every precinct, winning nearly twice as many votes as my five opponents combined.

Soon after my election I attended the opening of the new police academy in Hyde Park. The mayor was there to deliver some remarks. He spotted me in the audience. "You want to come up here and say a few words?" I shook my head. "Well, someday you're going to be up here speaking as mayor," said Kevin White, then in his last days in office.

> If you run for City Council two bad things can happen to you; one, you lose, two, you win.
>
> —*former congressman Barney Frank*

I'll spare you a chronicle of my ten years on the City Council. Instead, I'll fast-forward and tell how I got to be acting mayor.

It happened in two stages.

Stage one: I become chairman of the Ways and Means Committee.

First, I had to take the committee out of mothballs. For that I needed the help of the new mayor, Raymond Flynn.

Ray Flynn was one of the greatest athletes ever to come out of Boston. A multisport legend at South Boston High. An All-American basketball player at Providence College. A runner of road races and marathons well into his fifties.

Like me, Ray was a Hubert Humphrey Democrat. After his longshoreman father fell ill, his family had to go on welfare to survive. Ray never forgot that, and denounced President Reagan's cuts to the safety net as immoral.

Unlike me, Ray was colorful, riding on snowplows, driving to fires in his battered station wagon, hanging out at blue-collar taverns with cops and EMTs, and morning, noon, and night making news. An impossible act to follow as mayor, and I didn't try.

Ray began as a state legislator from South Boston, where he was a leader of that neighborhood's resistance to court-ordered busing to desegregate the Boston public schools. But Ray was never a white-backlash candidate like School Committee Chair Louise Day Hicks and City Councilor Albert "Dapper" O'Neil. As mayor he dedicated himself to healing the wounds left by busing. His "urban populism" stressed the economic common ground shared by working families of all races.

In 1978 he won a seat on the City Council and quickly grew fed up with the power of Ways and Means. "You'd just sit there, nine of you, and whoever was chair of Ways and Means, he would call the shots," he recalled years later. "If he was buddy-buddy with the mayor, you would have to [appeal to] him even if you wanted to ask questions. It was a joke." Ray pushed a reform under which, instead of Ways and Means overseeing the whole budget, twelve different committees monitored the budgets of the city departments. Ways and Means was mothballed.

On the council, I quickly grew fed up with Ray's "reform." Boston's city charter mandates a "strong mayor" form of government. As retiring incumbent John F. Collins allegedly told Kevin White in 1968, the mayor of Boston is a virtual emperor whose power rendered the Boston City Council "a band of eunuchs." The council cannot increase the city budget, originate bond issues or appropriations, or block the mayor's appointees to head city departments. It can approve or cut the mayor's budget. But under the twelve-committee system, oversight was spotty. Fifty-million-dollar appropriations were passed after ten-minute hearings.

My colleagues were bored with the financial details. Not me.

Mastering them as chair of a revived Ways and Means was my road up. But persuading Ray to reverse his stand would not be easy.

After I became mayor, one insider said, "It's almost safe to say that the last ten years was the Flynn-Menino administration." That's over the top. His second comment is correct: "Menino was the person Flynn went to in order to get things done on the Council."

I voted with Ray and tenants on condo (not condom) conversions, with him and gay rights activists on needle exchanges, with him and Irish Americans on a plan I worked out to buy the Jamaicaway mansion with the shamrock shutters built in 1915 by James Michael Curley.

And I strongly supported Ray's initiative to replace the elected Boston School Committee with a body appointed by the mayor. "This will be the piece that everybody judges Ray Flynn on," I said. "He's either going to be a great mayor or they are going to say, 'He couldn't turn the schools around.'" As mayor, I'd ask the voters to judge me by the same standard.

"Tommy used to come into my office and talk all the time," Ray once said. "More than all the other councilors put together. He was a team player. . . . You could trust him." Ray even asked me to join his team as parks commissioner. He did not see me, unknown outside my district, as competition. You have to be a politician to appreciate what that did for our relationship.

By late 1988 I'd carried enough water for Ray that he owed me. He knew how I felt about Ways and Means. "Let's have one committee," I said. Ray agreed. He weighed in with the council. And by a 9–3 vote, the council scrapped Ray's 1980 reform.

"A lot of us didn't realize how much more powerful it would make him," said Maura Hennigan, the council's only woman. She wasn't alone in having second thoughts about installing me as chair of Ways and Means. Ray Flynn didn't like it when I summoned his department heads to all-day hearings. Sometimes I'd catch a reporter dozing off and slam my gavel to wake him up. "I don't care how boring it is," I snapped at one. "If I have to stay awake, you have to stay awake." The *Globe* saluted my hard-bottom diligence: "If they gave a medal for all-round best councilor, it would be won by Menino, the Hyde Park workhorse who virtually carries the whole council in budget hearings."

Before, department heads ignored me. Now, they returned my calls.

I had given myself ten years on the council. Then up or out. My clock was ticking. When a mouse ran across my shoulders in my council office, it seemed like an omen.

I considered running for one of the four at-large seats on the council. Maybe my good press for holding officials' feet to the fire as chair of Ways and Means had increased my visibility. I commissioned a poll to find out. After Mayor Flynn and Laval Wilson, the superintendent of schools, I had the third-best job rating in the city, ahead of the other members of the City Council, the chair of the School Committee, and a state rep talked about as the next mayor. But what use was a good job rating if 60 percent of those polled had never heard of me?

Basically I was a stranger outside Hyde Park. I couldn't win an at-large seat on the council. Mayor? I didn't even consider it. Anyway, though Ray Flynn was flirting with running for governor in 1990, I was pretty sure he'd go for a third mayoral term in 1991 instead. The way up in city politics was blocked.

I explored a campaign for state treasurer or lieutenant governor. But the record wasn't encouraging. No one had jumped from City Council to state office since 1960. And there was this: "Menino could also have a problem with his public speaking style, which will not make anyone forget [the old-time orator] James Michael Curley," to quote a political columnist. I took speaking lessons. When you are giving a speech, one acting coach suggested, try wearing sneakers. "I can't take it anymore," I said, and quit.

Ahead of the '92 elections, a congressional seat unexpectedly opened. Brian Donnelly, longtime congressman from the Eleventh Congressional District, which covered southeastern Massachusetts, announced his retirement. My friends collected ten thousand signatures to get me on the ballot. At a once-shuttered Hyde Park paper mill that I'd help to reopen, I threw my hat into the ring.

A month later I snatched it back. Citing the 1990 census, a federal judge ruled that the Eleventh District had lost too much population to justify having a member of Congress. He ordered my part of the district merged with the newly configured Ninth District, a seat long held by Joe Moakley of South Boston. In challenging the dean of the Massachusetts congressional delegation, a bloody-minded journalist wrote, "Menino would be choosing to shoot and stab himself while garroting himself with piano wire." I quit *that* race.

These years weren't wasted politically.

I spent much of my time at community meetings in Hyde Park. "I just feel I have to be there," I told a reporter. "They elected me. If I'm able to help people through the bureaucracy, that's the best part of the job. . . . The way their lives go, my life goes."

My careful tending of the district paid off politically. I ran unopposed in 1989. But Hyde Park was a dead end for me. My poll had confirmed that. So, more and more, I ventured beyond the district. I held Ways and Means meetings in the neighborhoods, I visited health centers, I went to homeless shelters — I was out there learning the issues of the city.

To bolster my image as a neighborhood guy in my '83 campaign,

I played up not having a college degree. Cautioning me to rethink that tactic, Gerry Doherty picked up my father's banner: "If you don't have a college degree, you'll get stuck." That was my deepest fear.

So in 1984, at age forty-one, I enrolled in the College of Public and Community Service at the University of Massachusetts Boston. I never missed a class. I was afraid a fellow student would drop a dime to the media.

That same year my daughter Susan enrolled at UMass Amherst. During our first semester, I saw Gerry one day in City Hall. "Damn you, I had a terrible weekend because of you," I said. Startled, he asked why. "Well, my daughter is helping me with math. And my problem was, she stayed out late Saturday night and I had to ground her. So I was prepping for my math class on Monday and she refused to help me!"

> I've voted right on women's issues and I'll continue to vote right. Commitment to issues that are important to the city is what this should be about, not gender.
>
> —*on the challenge of running against a woman*

Stage two: I become council president.

It was bad timing, running against a woman in the "Year of the Woman." But the top job on the City Council was up for grabs, and my ten-year clock was about to strike midnight.

My opponent, Maura Hennigan, was endorsed by the Massachusetts Women's Political Caucus. The president of Massachusetts NOW vowed to unseat any councilor voting for me. Maura's candidacy was turned into the Boston edition of the backlash against the male-dominated politics on display during the Clarence Thomas–Anita Hill hearings. In the "Year of the Woman" elections of 1992, held while Maura and I were maneuvering for votes, the number of women tripled in the U.S. Senate and doubled in the House. The politicians on the Boston City Council took note.

The presidency was vacant because the councilor holding the office, a gentleman of the old school named Christopher Iannella, died in September 1992, touching off a four-month struggle to succeed him. The job was worth having, especially in 1993. Under the city charter, if the mayor died or resigned, the president of the council became acting mayor. Running as an incumbent, he or she would then be the favorite to win the special election to choose the new mayor.

Ray Flynn had over two years left in his term. But after nearly a decade as mayor, Ray was floating. With the Boston economy in recession, the job was harder than ever. Ray was a good-times mayor. Now that times were bad, he seemed to be looking for a way out of town. Washington beckoned. Word was Ray was in line for an appointment in the new Clinton administration.

Six of the thirteen councilors lined up with Maura. The press identified them as the "progressive" bloc. Six were more loosely aligned with me in the "conservative/moderate" bloc. The swing vote was Anthony Crayton, a new African American councilor from Roxbury.

The "progressive-versus-conservative" labeling confused what was really going on. "What's a progressive? I'm more liberal than most of the progressives," I said, pointing to my votes on homelessness, AIDS, and other issues. As I saw it, ideology wasn't driving the progressives. Political ambition was. Four of Maura's six wanted to be mayor. They assumed I did, too. (It was a safe assumption.) They knew the next council president might vault to acting mayor. And they did not want me to be the one.

Through the last weeks of 1992, Crayton came under pressure to vote for Maura. Black and Hispanic leaders had pushed the council to approve a new minority district in Jamaica Plain. But the chair of the Redistricting Committee, Jimmy Kelly of South Boston, opposed it. Kelly was one of my six. The Black Political Task Force put Crayton on notice: A vote for me as president was a vote for Kelly as chairman. "The decision Tony Crayton makes will almost certainly be a career decision," said the president of the task force. "There will be a lot of progressive forces that will support another candidate for that seat."

But Tony, a hardworking member of Ways and Means, was ambitious. He wanted to replace me as committee chair, believing he could advance minority interests from that post. The council president appoints the chairs. I didn't have to spell it out. If Tony backed me for president, I'd name him chair.

Hennigan thought that neither of us would get seven votes on the first ballot, giving her a chance to lure one of the three conservatives away from me. That strategy might have worked. The conservatives were livid with me for voting to override Ray Flynn's veto of a bill that required most city restaurants to install condom vending machines — this after I supported, opposed, and supported it again! My coalition almost broke down. "I'm really getting beat up," I told a reporter, who wrote that I "seemed likely to lose" my bid for the presidency. One of the conservatives might have voted "present" to punish me, or held off for a ballot to see what Maura had to offer. But the progressives behind Maura barely talked to the conservatives. I listened to them and would work with them.

Respect — shown by hearing people out and disagreeing without being disagreeable — is a vanishing political virtue. When I was new on the council, and the papers would quote me criticizing the mayor, my father would call me up to complain: "Don't say things like that about the mayor. You have to show him some respect." Carl

Menino may have hated politics, but from him I learned the secret that kept my coalition together. Hours before the vote, the conservatives met behind closed doors and decided to go for me on the first ballot.

"It is heartening that a well-qualified candidate prevailed," the *Globe* wrote of my 7–6 victory in an editorial titled "A Comer as Council President." Black and Hispanic leaders who lumped me in with the "conservatives" could take comfort from these words in the editorial: "Since his district encompasses Hyde Park and Roslindale, two racially mixed neighborhoods, [Menino] has an acute sense of the changes that are transforming the city and a knack for reconciling newcomers and longtime residents."

Maura was gracious in defeat. "It would have been wonderful to win, but it didn't happen," she said. "You live to fight another day." That would be a long time coming.

> The neighbors crowded round for a block party in the Readville section. Neat little bungalows, cheek by jowl, emptied as hot dogs, pizza and soft drinks disappeared. The new mayor gave a Readville-is-now-on-the map speech, and he danced in the street with Angela while somebody's stereo blared Sinatra's "My Way."
>
> —*from David Nyhan's column in the* Boston Globe, *July 20, 1993*

In early March, Ray Flynn summoned me to the mayor's office. Bill Clinton had asked him to be U.S. ambassador to the Vatican. Should he take the job? "Mayor" (never "Ray"), I said, "some of us from the neighborhoods might get to be congressmen, but name anyone from South Boston or Hyde Park who ever got to be an ambassador. Take it." Ray said he'd mull Rome over. His call came at 2:30 in the afternoon: "Go out and get some new suits; you're going to be acting mayor."

"My whole life has changed in a matter of twenty-four hours," I said to reporters during a flying visit with Ray to Doyle's, a politico haunt in Jamaica Plain. "What's important is not the political future of Tom Menino; it's the future of the city."

Adrian Walker of the *Globe* wouldn't let me get away with that pious pose: "But even as he declared that government, not politics, comes first, Menino was moving to set up a campaign for November. While Menino worked his way around Doyle's—pressing the flesh in a crowd that seemed far more interested in Flynn—veteran political strategist Edward Jesser, a Menino friend for 25 years, was sequestered in the restaurant's office, recruiting campaign workers and planning fund-raising."

I sent that clip to Ed Jesser and asked if it "rings a bell." He wrote back, "I remember it well." His recollection reads like a scene from *The Last Hurrah,* the classic novel about Boston politics, and politics everywhere:

> I entered a few seconds before you to watch the crowd carefully. The place was mobbed. . . . Having spent the previous ten years as a regular of Doyle's, a stomping ground for Flynn, his senior staff, and Globies, I knew the crowd well. I was interested in those who barely acknowledged or ignored the current mayor but pressed close to and bestowed congratulations on Your Incipience. Our future campaign workers. I braced them, confirmed their liking of the future acting mayor and moved it from support to pledges with ease. You were standing ten feet away and they had to tell me they were not with you to avoid my little whirlpool. A difficult task if you had to or wished to curry the favorable opinion of the next mayor. . . . Adrian [Walker] caught me not long after in Eddie Burke's office using much of this information to enhance the Menino landslide, explain the train was leaving the station, preclude the anti-Menino idea of needing a meeting to decide on a favorite candidate, and, yes, begin arranging fund raisers. . . . It

was a good day, a veritable wonderland for political operative and writer alike. . . . It rings a bell.

That was in March 1993. The U.S. Senate was scheduled to act on Ray's nomination in May. Everybody assumed he'd be sworn in quickly as ambassador and resign as mayor. Technically, he had until July 12. Any later than that and city law required that the special election in November be for the remaining two years of Ray's term, not for a full four-year term.

Ray blew hot and cold for weeks. He couldn't be any old ambassador to the Holy See. He had to bring his message of "social and economic justice" to the poor everywhere. Ray Flynn had to be ambassador to the world.

Rule-bound and bureaucratic, the State Department was overmatched with Ray, who as emperor of Boston made the rules. No such posting as roving ambassador exists, they told him. Then create one, Ray said.

While Ray fiddled, Boston politics burned. Six candidates declared for mayor: four members of the City Council, the sheriff of Suffolk County, and a state legislator from Dorchester. A former police commissioner and a former TV news anchor would soon join the mix. A marathon of seventy-six forums and debates stretching to the September preliminary election began. Often, we wound up talking to each other's sign holders. By the end I was so tired that, sitting through another candidate's speech for the fifty-seventh time, I dozed off and fell out of my chair.

The campaign was three months old when Ray called the six candidates to a hurry-up meeting at the Parkman House, the city-owned mansion on Beacon Hill, to deliver the bad news: He might stay on as mayor of Boston. Rome just wasn't working out. None of us could speak.

The next day the mayor made a dramatic announcement: He would go to Rome. Ray had used the Parkman House meeting to jam a decision out of State. To avoid weeks of damaging Ray-inspired leaks, it caved to most of his demands. We candidates were stage props in his play.

It was now June. I had hoped to be acting mayor. I could not talk the job. I had to be mayor to be elected mayor. That was my strategy. Ray was trashing it. Every day he hung on at City Hall was a day less to show my stuff.

Meanwhile, the voters had forgotten me. "Where Is Tom Menino?" a *Globe* headline inquired. Menino signs were "as rare as Red Sox victories." I was "overshadowed" in a series of debates. I "laid an egg" doing stand-up at a comedy club. I was "a bit frayed in the syntax department." A must-read columnist offered a backhanded compliment: "Tom Menino is no actor. He's built like a longshoreman, talks like a truck driver, and works like a mule." Notices like that hurt my fundraising. They demoralized my volunteers. My campaign was going nowhere.

Then events began breaking my way. On the last day of June, Ray was confirmed as ambassador to the Holy See by the Senate. On July 9 Ray was sworn in by Vice President Al Gore. Ray had until five P.M. on the twelfth to resign.

How did I stay sane that day in City Hall? Ray and his wife, Cathy, were booked on an evening flight to Rome — but Ray was missing. His staff did not know where he was. His police detail was in the dark. A friend reported seeing him slip out of the building in his running clothes.

In my fifth-floor council office, we awaited Ray's return.

We — Angela, my two kids, my brother, some friends, and the journalist Dave Nyhan, the one who said I worked like a mule —

spent the time nervously reminiscing while Ray took his last run as mayor through the neighborhoods. Good thing Boston was only forty-four square miles.

I recalled my father's reaction to the big news of a decade before:

ME: I'm gonna run for City Council.

CARL: You got two children and a wife to support. What if you lose?

ME: Dad, I won't lose.

CARL: Give me a break! You're gonna win?

ME: Dad, I'm gonna win.

Angela remembered being miserable during that first race in 1983. She'd been with me through two lost jobs. There was no guarantee my old job at the State House would be waiting for me. I was over forty. Most men were secure in their careers by then. I was *trying* to start over. True, the kids were grown, and she had a good job as a bookkeeper. With her salary we could cover the note on our $35,000 house. But we'd relied on my job for health insurance. And neither of us could expect much of a pension. I knew all that, but she knew the details of every dollar spent and made sure they always stretched far enough. She also knew how much I liked to shop, and eat. Not wanting to dampen my spirits, she kept her thoughts to herself.

Left unsaid, as we waited for Ray to return from his run, was that her anxiety then was a preview of her anxiety now. If I lost the mayor's race, I'd be out of a job. And this time I was fifty.

At 4:20 a phone rang in the outer office. We all stopped talking at once. A moment later a staffer opened the door. "That was the clerk's office," he said. "He signed the letter. It's down there."

I led our little band into the cement slab corridor ("like a racquetball court," I'd later describe my office walls) and through a parting of reporters and cameramen to the mayor's office. Ray was there, having his picture taken with the last of a long line of well-wishers.

In a 2009 interview with Joe Keohane of *Boston Magazine,* Ray gave his version of what happened next: "The day I was in my office leaving, I was asked by his staff . . . if I would say something very positive about Tommy before all the press. I said, 'Look, I know [mayoral candidates] Jimmy Brett and Mickey Roache. Those guys were friends of mine and I don't want to be dictating who the next mayor is going to be. . . .' 'Well, can you say something like, the city is in good hands?' So I said, 'Sure, I can say that.' Of course that's the front page headline, with a picture of Tommy Menino. They asked me if I could hug him [for the photo]. So I did."

The ask to say something positive—I knew about that. But nobody cleared the hug with me.

> I often wish God had given me the silver tongue of Mario Cuomo, the looks of Bill Clinton, and the golf swing of Jack Nicklaus. But he didn't. He did give me a big heart, a gift for numbers, and a love for the city of Boston.
>
> —*speaking at a candidates' forum in 1993*

The first poll appeared on my second day in office. It killed the joy. With eight weeks to go before the September preliminary, I trailed the front-runner by 10 points. She was my council colleague Rosaria Salerno, a former Benedictine nun and a staunch progressive channeling "Year of the Woman" energy with her campaign slogan, "Not One of the Boys."

In what was now a seven-candidate race, she had a big lead. But the votes weren't there to elect her in a two-person race. In city elections, held in off years, half those who vote in presidential election years don't show up. The missing were Rosaria's voters—young, single, well educated, progressive, gay—living in the low-voting wards of Allston, Mission Hill, the Fenway, the Back Bay, and the South End. In city elections the votes were in South Boston, West Roxbury, Dorchester, and Hyde Park. The candidate opposing her in the final would clean up in those neighborhoods, which don't vote on ideology—"progressive" or "conservative"—but on the delivery of city services like police, fire, trash collection, and the like. Those were my issues. I wanted to be that candidate.

The acting mayor needed to start acting like a mayor. Days after taking over, I reprogrammed $500,000 from the city's reserve fund to put kids to work in summer jobs. "It gets you up early in the morning," I told them, "and when you get home at night you're too tired to get into trouble on the streets." It was the beginning of something big.

Every year, starting in January, I'd appeal to the civic spirit of executives from the banks, the tech firms, the hospitals, and the insurance companies. With your help, I'd say, we can make this a safe summer in Boston. Hire as many kids as you can. Give them a break . . . We started with one hundred businesses and institutions, and ended with three hundred, including major employers like John Hancock, State Street Bank, and Brigham and Women's Hospital.

The city did its part, too. Every year I'd set aside several million dollars to pay kids $8 an hour to clean up parks and tourist sites like the Freedom Trail. Ten thousand kids every summer—that was the goal. In tight years, budget watchdogs complained that the city couldn't afford to hire several thousand kids, and I'd respond, "This isn't about today. This is about tomorrow," and the city hired the kids. Over twenty years I pulled together $150 million in city, state, and federal money to fund more than 200,000 summer jobs.

All the kids got experience earning—and managing—their own

money. Those who showed up and did the work got a good reference from their supervisors. Some kids learned the lesson I took away from my summer job at Bird & Sons. I shared it with Shirley Leung, a business columnist at the *Globe*, for a piece she wrote about the Mayor's Summer Jobs program: "You have to work hard to make . . . money. You have to get dirty." A lucky few were offered full-time jobs after they graduated from high school. Leung interviewed a young woman named Icandace Woods, who turned a city-arranged summer internship at the Dana-Farber Cancer Institute into a career as a clinical team leader. "These [summer] jobs are amazing," she told Leung. "It [gives] us hope and shows that someone cares."

And people ask me why I got into politics.

So, bringing Hyde Park values to City Hall, I said yes on summer jobs. Yes on putting police cadets in station houses to free up more cops for the streets. Yes on redeploying officers to a new Youth Violence Strike Force. But to show I was tough enough to be mayor, I also had to say no.

My pollster, Irwin "Tubby" Harrison, discovered a potential breakout issue from focus group interviews with Boston residents. Some were angry about unsafe streets and others about failing schools, parking, or trash pickup. But all of them were furious over their water bills.

To pay for the decade-long cleanup of Boston Harbor, home owners had seen their water bills rise overnight from a nominal yearly sum to hundreds of dollars a quarter with no end in sight. The bills were sent by the Boston Water and Sewer Commission, an appointed body beyond the voters' reach. The mayor picked the three members of the commission board. I asked one of Ray's holdover lawyers if I could order the board to freeze the rates for a year. The law was murky, but the lawyer doubted I had the power. "Can't do it?" I interrupted. "Want to bet?"

I announced the freeze in the morning. On the TV news at noon, City Councilor John Nucci, until recently one of my competitors in the mayor's race, said I lacked the authority to freeze the rates. On the six o'clock news he hailed the freeze as a relief for hard-pressed home owners paying for the wasteful, crony-laden sewer commission. Between noon and six, irate constituents had flooded his office with calls. John's turnabout was a test of the water rates issue. It was a winner. "It's Tommy's week," an anonymous councilor told the *Globe*.

Freezing the rates became our rallying cry in the preliminary and general election campaigns. Hit again and again in television ads. Pounded home in speeches, debates, and media interviews. A textbook example of entrepreneurial politics: Find a voting issue unexploited by your opponents and make it your own. We veterans of the three Timilty-White fights, of Jimmy Carter's '76 and '80 campaigns, of my '83 and subsequent council campaigns — we old hands knew how to play this game.

An August poll showed Rosaria falling from 22 percent to 19 percent. She was stuck on gender. Too late, she realized that her pitch — vote for me because I'm "not one of the boys" — wasn't giving people enough reason to vote for her. She was also battling the prejudice against electing women to executive office. And she misread the mood of the voters in attacking me as "Kevin Flynn," as if balancing downtown development with neighborhood services was somehow unprogressive. As Ray Flynn himself said, Boston had moved on from the anti-downtown politics of 1983. In a slumping economy, people wanted a "Kevin Flynn" for mayor.

The same poll had me stuck at 14 percent. But I was confident my numbers would rise after the rate freeze. It was popular in itself. Who wants to pay a higher water bill? And it showed me acting like a mayor.

Another mayoral moment came in September, two weeks before the preliminary. The School Committee agreed to a new teachers' contract. I said, "Go back to the bargaining table and get a better deal for the city."

Dave Nyhan scored it a win for me. "Everybody used to make fun of the way you talk," he wrote. "So you lose a few 'g's' here and there. People hereabouts talk like you talk. Nothing fancy. But when you got the chance to say 'no' [on the teachers' contract] you said it loud and clear. Can Menino handle the job? No question. Case closed." Fifty-eight percent of the voters agreed.

Soon, FOR MAYOR MENINO signs sprouted in yards across the city, exploiting the magic of incumbency in Boston elections. Flyers in sixteen languages conveyed my commitment to safe neighborhoods, good schools, and caring government.

As Rosaria lost ground, Jim Brett gained it. A veteran state legislator representing white Dorchester, Jim was at home in neighborhood taverns and downtown boardrooms, an articulate, attractive candidate and a very good guy.

Those were some of Jim's positives. There were three negatives.

First, although he was a player at the State House, Jim had no name recognition outside Dorchester. Second, he was a close friend of a controversial politician, State Senate President William "Billy" Bulger of South Boston, brother of the famous gangster "Whitey" Bulger. Brett argued that his ties to Billy Bulger would benefit the city. But the Bulger association, which extended through Jim's wife, who worked for Bulger for twenty years, was a burden to Brett, especially in the minority community, where Bulger's anti-busing politics of the 1970s was not forgotten or, like Ray Flynn's, forgiven. Third, Jim's down-the-line Catholic opposition to abortion, an issue not relevant to city politics, gave this work-and-wages Democrat an undeserved reputation for conservatism. Progressive and minority voters got the impression that he would not be a mayor for *them.*

Balancing these negatives was a big cultural positive. Since 1925 Boston had elected seven mayors. All were Irish Americans. So was Jim Brett. The Irish voted above their falling weight in the population: "Heavy-voting ward" was ethnically neutral shorthand for an Irish American neighborhood. Jim Brett was of Irish descent. Former news anchor Christopher Lydon topped that, boasting that he was the only Irish *citizen* in the race. Mickey Roache, Ray Flynn's former police commissioner, wanted it known that he received the Blessed Sacrament seven days a week.

By the 1980s Italian Americans my age were tired of the "Pick-a-Mick" choice of mayors on the ballot and for once wanted to vote for one of their own. I learned that walking house-to-house in my '83 council race. A man would come to the door, notice the name on my campaign button, and say, "Menino? I'm with ya. I'm Russo." When I addressed Italian American audiences in '93, it wasn't my charisma that excited them. The green tide in Boston politics was receding, and Italians weren't the only group standing on the beach happy to see it go.*

> Come November 3rd — the day after you elect me mayor — the city of Boston will begin a new era in which the needs of families are given the highest priority.
>
> —*from a speech delivered the night the election became a two-man race*

* The tide flowed back in the November 2013 election pitting Martin J. Walsh against John R. Connolly. However, in the September preliminary election, the candidates included an African American woman who had served in my administration, a Hispanic city councilor, a Jewish city councilor, and a former school committeeman from a Cape Verdean immigrant family.

The winners of the September preliminary were . . . me, with 27 percent of the vote, and Jim Brett, with 23 percent. Rosaria Salerno, with 17 percent, was out of the running.

Boston would not have its first woman mayor, but it was likely to see its first Italian American one. Polls showed me with a big lead.

The swing vote was nearly all to Jim Brett's left. It was now my vote. One poll showed me running 28 points ahead among "liberals" and, reflecting my support for abortion rights, 19 points ahead among women. It didn't help Jim that Bishop John Patrick Boles picked this moment to endorse him.

I had a good record on gay issues but, unlike Salerno, I had not supported domestic partner benefits for city employees. That did not matter to the Greater Boston Lesbian and Gay Political Alliance. It did not matter when, in a speech to them, I came out for "the distribution of condominiums." I wasn't Jim Brett. They endorsed me.

When Roache called for an end to affirmative action in the Boston Police Department, I said, "We have to have a police department that reflects the diversity of the city." Salerno, Sheriff Robert Ruffo, City Councilor Bruce Bolling, and Lydon had all taken the same position. Only Brett, "who hails from conservative Dorchester, remained ambiguous on the issue," the *Globe* reported. Then at a meeting held in a Roxbury church, Brett, normally a careful speaker, referred to "you people." This was a year after Ross Perot, addressing the Urban League, had created a furor by speaking of "your people." The Roxbury audience seemed shocked. "Condominiums" for "condoms" revealed my struggle with language. "You people," to African Americans, betrayed contempt. In this context it wasn't surprising that Bolling, the only African American in the race, now endorsed me. So did Mel King, the civil rights legend who ran against Ray Flynn in 1983.

Jim's chances of winning were fading fast. A question in our last debate destroyed them. A *Herald* columnist quoted a Brett campaign slogan calling Jim "a forceful, intelligent voice for Boston." Picking up on the implied contrast, he asked, "Do you consider yourself more intelligent and articulate than Mr. Menino?" Jim, sensing danger in sounding superior, objected: "I find that question rather insulting. I have never said that and I know Tom would never say that." The debate was held before a large audience at the Boston Public Library, and there was a rush of applause for Jim. Yet the idea that Jim's slogan was slyly equating my thick tongue with a thick head was out there.

It wasn't as if I was hiding my difficulties as a public speaker. My TV ads included the line "I'm not a fancy talker" (pronounced "talkah"), "but I get the job done." And in interviews I was careful to say things like "Hey, I'm not the best-looking guy in the world and I know nobody is ever going to ask me to host *Masterpiece Theatre.*" And then add: "But mayors don't get paid by the word. You can't talk a playground into being clean."

Well before Election Day someone was stapling R.I.P. on Brett lawn signs in West Roxbury. As voters went to the polls, the only question was the size of my victory margin. It was bigger than I expected: 28 points. Eighteen of the city's twenty-two wards.

My one regret was that my friend Tony Crayton, who'd put me first in line to be acting mayor, lost his council seat by 80 votes. "I gave him his dream to be mayor," he said. Credit was also due to another politician, and when just before midnight he called to congratulate me, I gave it: "Thank you, Mr. President, for making the mayor ambassador."

Brett later said he thought he was running for an open seat: "But what happened when Tom became acting mayor changed the race.

I didn't see that coming." He was running against an incumbent, a sitting mayor. The last one to lose was Curley, in 1949, when he was old, sick, and lately returned from federal prison.

Ray Flynn knew why Jim Brett lost. It happened the day I became acting mayor and Ray said he was leaving the city in good hands and the media treated it like an endorsement and the cameras zoomed in on the hug: "Jimmy Brett was upset with me for that.... I heard him say it cost him the election."

The five thousand friends and supporters attending my inaugural party at the Hynes Convention Center were entertained by representatives of the New America—multiracial, multicultural, LGBT-friendly—rising in the old city. A Roma band performed, followed by two groups of Irish step dancers and a gay country and western dance troupe and actors from the Ramón de los Reyes Spanish Dance Theatre and performers illustrating "The Art of Black Dance and Music." Sandy Martin sang a selection of songs from *The Best of Patsy Cline.* There was a woodwind quintet. We were treated to a Chinese lion dance. I missed a Frank Sinatra karaoke, but nobody asked me.

The next morning I delivered my inaugural address at Faneuil Hall. Angela introduced me. She described my mother's efforts on behalf of new immigrants. And listening to her, I reflected that the truest line in my speech was "I am here because of my family."

I wasn't there because I'd been in politics longer than the six other contenders combined—not because, since that day at Kelly Field when I met Joe Timilty, I had played a central role in over a dozen campaigns, including four for mayor of Boston. I wasn't there because of my decade on the City Council, although I knew the people and problems in every department of city government. I wasn't there because of my vision, which wasn't that different from the other candidates'. And although I declared, "I'm the luckiest guy in the world," I wasn't there because of my luck, the miracle that transformed the shy guy, the mediocre student, "Mumbles" into the mayor.

I was there because of my family. Because of the values passed on from my parents — treat everyone with respect, help others, work hard, sacrifice for your children. To this inheritance I added sympathy with the struggles of ordinary Americans. I think people wanted a ready heart in their mayor. Regardless, they got one.

Angela introduced the theme of my speech — my vision of Hyde Park for all. I called the roll of my memories. My grandmother and grandfather with their stories of the hard life in Grottaminarda. The aunts and uncles and cousins they brought here to make their start in America. The inspiring image of Susan Menino, and of Carl Menino nearly felled by her loss. "The Deacon" walking the beat. The Westinghouse plant. The neighborhood. "You know," I said, "when I grew up on Hyde Park Ave, we knew everybody who lived there. Now I live in Readville and don't know my next-door neighbor. Angela works, I work. . . . Can we recover that closeness in our neighborhoods? I think we can." The simple things that make up a good life . . . I wanted them for everybody. In a twenty-minute speech, I used "promise" nineteen times.

I ended with a bow to the Irish American political tradition in Boston, the green tide that washed over the city from Mayor Hugh O'Brien in 1884 to Mayor John F. Fitzgerald in 1906 to his grandson Congressman John F. Kennedy in 1946 and on up through Kevin Hagan White in 1968 and "my predecessor and friend" Ray Flynn in 1984. "But this is a new day," I said, turning the page of history onto the majority-minority city of the twenty-first century, the Boston of the Haitian, Puerto Rican, Cape Verdean, Somali, Chinese, Vietnamese, and other immigrants whose names in the list of future mayors will look as familiar as Fitzgerald and Flynn do to us. I paused to take in the rows of officials and friends cramming the Great Hall back to the outsize doors hung on iron hinges forged by blacksmiths in Paul Revere's day. Memory supplied the thirteen granite steps (one for each of the colonies) that JFK had descended thirty-three years earlier and the cobblestone street where I had started the long run that returned me to this place as mayor of Boston. There was no need to look down at the text. I knew the next lines by heart: "I am the first Italian American to hold this job. Am I proud of that? You bet I am."

UP FROM BUSING

> Q. What issue is so personal to you, so important, that you'll never change your opinion on it, no matter what?
> A. Racism. I will not tolerate it. . . . That's the interesting thing about my life. I was in the first grade — I will always remember this. It's only a little thing, but I always remember it. . . . My name is spelled M-E-N-I-N-O, unlike the "Manino" that's on the mushroom jar. . . . And the first-grade teacher told me that my parents didn't know how to spell my name — that Italians couldn't spell. So she changed the spelling. And I went through the first grade with my name spelled wrong. . . . That's a little thing. But it's always stayed with me. . . . And I will never tolerate people being discriminated against.
>
> —*from an interview with me, then acting mayor, in the* Boston Globe, *July 22, 1993*

For her first question in my first national television interview as mayor, Katie Couric asked: "You know, many people view Boston as the most racially divided city in the country. Do you think that reputation is deserved?"

"Oh, no," I said, that perception was out of date—the city had moved on. But I knew she was right.

Boston got that reputation during "busing," the school desegregation crisis of the 1970s. I served in the trenches of busing as a monitor at Hyde Park High, trying to keep black and white kids from fighting. I saw enough ugliness in those hallways to make me cry for my city.

In June 1974 a federal judge, Arthur W. Garrity, ruled that the Boston School Committee had deliberately segregated the city's public schools. Using a plan thought up by professors of education, he ordered eighteen thousand students bused from segregated to integrated schools starting in September.

The plan paired Roxbury, the center of African American life in Boston, with South Boston, the center of white resistance to "forced busing." South Boston kids would be bused to Roxbury, Roxbury kids to South Boston.

It did not go unnoticed that this pairing was crazy.

One professor urged the judge to leave Southie out of the first year of the plan because of its "intense hostility to blacks." Another professor countered that racial hostility had not been allowed to frustrate integration in the South and shouldn't be allowed to in South Boston. Judge Garrity sided with him.

"We're being punished for what we are," said one of South Boston's state legislators, Michael Flaherty. The professors saw the Southie protesters as racists. The protesters saw themselves as defenders of their neighborhood schools against an unelected judge bent on destroying them.

If the judge had listened to the first professor, busing might not have sparked so much resistance elsewhere in the city. On the first day of classes, in most of the eighty schools affected by the plan, things went comparatively smoothly. TV news, however, focused on Southie, on the angry crowds and the graffiti (KILL NIGGERS, KKK) *on the walls of South Boston High. And the spirit of Southie spread.*

Southie experienced the worst violence. But there was plenty to go around. At Hyde Park High a white kid was stabbed, touching off a racial brawl in the cafeteria. Shortly after, police arrested four white kids driving near the school with Molotov cocktails in their car.

Outside Hyde Park High School, City Councilor Albert "Dapper" O'Neil showed up one day to troll for the hate vote. "I'm not going to stand by and let those niggers take over this school," he told a reporter.

Boston "got" a reputation for racism in the busing years? No, Boston earned it.

Busing was intended to end school segregation, but it promoted resegregation with only a brief stop at integration. Schools that were 40 percent minority in 1970 were nearly 90 percent minority two decades later. The 1980 census revealed that a third of white and black families with children under eighteen had fled the city. Eight thousand fewer people lived in South Boston and thirteen thousand fewer in Roxbury. Support for Garrity's plan among blacks had fallen to 14 percent.

Busing left Boston's schools segregated by race and class. By 1990, nine in ten students were eligible for free lunches. Six in ten school families made less than $15,000 a year.

Some kids, we discovered, had nothing. Before Christmas 1995, I started a toy drive. On Christmas Eve we walked up Geneva Avenue in Dorchester, handing out toys and clothes donated by Boston retailers and gift-wrapped by volunteers working outside my office at City Hall. A member of my staff, Mike Keneavy, knocked on one door. A little boy appeared. His mother wasn't home, he said. She was out getting his present at McDonald's. Only Mike's Santa act kept him from choking up. The Geneva Avenue walk became a Christmas tradition. So did the toy drive. By my last year in office we were delivering toys to four thousand families.

You can debate whether busing was a justified remedy for Boston's separate and unequal schools. You can't debate whether this experiment in instant social change failed. Busing left me with lasting doubts about "sweeping solutions," "bold plans," and "fundamental transformations" for the problems of city life.

Today a Dapper O'Neil, who praised Alabama governor George C. Wallace in the City Council, called Boston's growing Asian community "gooks," and campaigned with Ronald Reagan, couldn't be elected dogcatcher in Boston.

The career of the man who finally unseated Dapper on the City Council reveals the distance Boston has traveled since busing. Michael Flaherty ran against me for mayor in 2009 on a ticket with Sam Yoon, a Korean American lawyer. In 2008 Flaherty campaigned in the Massachusetts primary for Senator Barack Obama. Yet Michael Flaherty is from South Boston, where his father led the respectable anti-busing forces in the 70s and thugs stoned buses carrying black children.

Today Boston is a different city.

I'm as certain of that as I am of the spelling of my own name. So I couldn't believe my ears when the two candidates competing to replace me as mayor were asked in a TV debate if there was racism in the Boston Police Department and City Councilor John R. Connolly said, "There's racism in all of Boston, systemic, institutional, and structural." State Representative Martin J. Walsh agreed: "We have racism in the city of Boston that we have to deal with. We talk about one Boston, but we don't see one Boston in the city of Boston right now."

I wanted to shout: You guys don't know what racism is! You should have walked the hallways of Hyde Park High back in the day.

I simmered down when I saw what the candidates were doing: appealing to the swing vote in the election. It's a sign of progress that Boston's minority voters have such clout. Another sign: In winning the November 2013 election, Marty Walsh carried both South Boston and Roxbury. Racial polarization, white against black, gave Boston its bad name. Walsh's biracial vote shows that's history.

In Boston blacks are still likelier than whites to be poor or unemployed, to be discriminated against in housing and employment, to drop out of school, and to be victims of violent crime. Boston is part of America.

But it matters that for twenty years Boston had a mayor committed to lifting the cloud of racism over the city. A mayor who brought people together, reached out, and spoke out. A mayor who appointed persons of color to positions of power. A mayor who steered resources to Roxbury, Dorchester, and Mattapan. A mayor who moved the city forward on race.

Don't take my word for it. Listen to an authority, Celtics legend Bill Russell, who battled racism during his long career in Boston. "Today," he told the press in 2004, "we see a Boston that is making every effort to be one of our country's most inclusive and progressive cities under the leadership of Mayor Menino."

Here are two factual outlines of the difference my mayoralty made to Boston's communities of color. One traces the revival of a neighborhood; the other describes my frustration with a governor caught between his promise to locate a state office building in Roxbury and his ambition for higher office.

The neighborhood was Grove Hall, on the Roxbury-Dorchester border. When I was a kid, my parents would drive the four miles of Blue Hill Avenue from Mattapan Square to buy fresh-baked bread and rolls at Kasanoff's Bakery in Grove Hall. It was a thriving commercial dis-

trict, with movie theaters, delicatessens, kosher butcher shops, and a supermarket. Two riots in the 60s, one following Martin Luther King's assassination, left it a boarded-up shell.

Driving through Roxbury with Angela after becoming mayor, I said, "You know, all I want to do as mayor is to make Roxbury as good as West Roxbury," one of Boston's nicest residential neighborhoods. The day after I was elected, I took a victory lap around the city to thank the voters. First stop, Grove Hall. In my inaugural and through my first year, I pledged: "We're going to bring it back to where it was, a neighborhood that has economic development and hope for the people who live there. No, it won't have Kasanoff's Bakery. But we'll have smaller businesses, we'll have residences . . . we'll bring people back to that place." I was sticking my neck out: "If this works it will be one of the showpieces of my administration. If it doesn't, it will be one of my big failures."

I'll tell the Grove Hall story quickly, but it unfolded as change does in cities — slowly.

The city owned a hundred parcels of abandoned land along Blue Hill Avenue. I began there. In 1994 I promised to turn fifty of them over to developers within a year and fill at least half of those properties with new businesses within two years. In the meantime, to "show somebody cares," we put up white picket fences in front of the vacant lots.

Blue Hill Ave was pocked with run-down apartment buildings. The landlords lived in the suburbs. So we ran ads in their local newspapers, listing their names and describing the condition of their properties. We headed the ads "House of Shame."

Entrepreneurs wanting to start businesses in Grove Hall needed capital. The banks said no. The city said yes — first to the Big Load Laundry, then to a single mom who, with a $500,000 loan from the city, opened Grove Hall's first sit-down restaurant in years. She had no *collateral but, as I explained, "she showed enthusiasm and drive. You have to have faith in people."*

With "empowerment zone" money from Bill Clinton's Department of Housing and Urban Development combined with state and city funds, we built 150 units of new and renovated housing on the side streets off Blue Hill Ave. The Globe liked the "suburban feel" of these "modern, well-kept homes."

Over the objections of developers who wanted the land, I sited a $7.2 million early education center at the edge of the Grove Hall business district. A reporter tagged along while I showed off the center's "handsome brick exterior and the state-of-the-art interior, with wooden floors, easy-to-maintain carpets and flexible, modular classroom layout."

The center was the area's largest single investment until the 2001 opening of the $10 million Grove Hall Retail Mall, a project nurtured for a decade by the local Neighborhood Development Corporation. The tenants included CVS, Dunkin' Donuts, and a fifteen-thousand-square-foot Stop & Shop supermarket, something last seen in these parts in the 1960s. Today a $9 million seventy-one-unit housing complex fills Kasanoff's old space.

"People are actually moving back into the community, people who left reluctantly at a point where they had no hope," the director of a local nonprofit said in 1996. "Now they're saying, 'I can come home.'" And we were just getting started . . .

I kept my promise to Roxbury. Mitt Romney broke his.

From 1991 to 2006, Massachusetts had four Republican governors. Three of them understood that without Boston, Massachusetts is New Hampshire. They got it that Boston is the engine of the state economy. Three of them indicated that, when the time was right, they would help renew a lagging Boston neighborhood by moving a major state department there. The fourth Republican governor, Mitt Romney, sounded like he got it: "I believe great cities are a key to a great state."

The one thousand employees of the Massachusetts Department of Public Health were scattered across five separate facilities in Boston. Consolidating them in one headquarters made budgetary sense. Siting that building in Dudley Square made economic and social sense.

Dudley Square is at the heart of Roxbury. Like Grove Hall, it had never recovered from the 60s. But, partly on spillover commerce from nearby Grove Hall, by 2003 it was showing signs of life. The plywood covering the square's nineteenth-century buildings had come off. Restaurants were opening. An old hotel was being restored.

But Dudley's recovery could not gain momentum so long as a huge blighted building stood in the middle of the square. Ferdinand's Blue Store, once one of the Northeast's leading furniture retailers, closed in the 60s, and the 1898 building had been vacant ever since, discouraging investment in Dudley Square.

In 1998, after years of pressure from my office and from Roxbury politicians and nonprofits, the state legislature voted to build a $70 million 200,000-square-foot DPH headquarters at the Ferdinand's site.

Delayed, the project was teed up for Romney when he took office in 2003. Merchants were adjusting business plans to handle the estimated $2 million annually in new trade. Big media events at Dudley Square had raised expectations. A neighborhood that had known no hope for decades knew hope now.

Then Governor Romney found reasons to back out. Downtown rents were falling. The number of DPH employees was shrinking. The department might disappear in his restructuring of state government. There was an economic crisis, a budget squeeze . . .

My development experts pointed out that rents would rise when the economy recovered. That, compared to the cost of its leases downtown, *the state would save $500 million annually over the twenty years of its lease with the city in Dudley Square—and then own the building outright.*

But Mitt Romney wasn't thinking long-term and he wasn't thinking of Massachusetts. For him the State House was a steppingstone to the White House. He did not run for reelection as governor in 2006 but for the GOP nomination for president in 2008. He'd seen Massachusetts as a springboard since he challenged Senator Ted Kennedy in 1994.

Teddy was in trouble that year. He called me. "I need your help," he said. He got it. The turning point in the campaign was his debate with Romney at Faneuil Hall. Romney was like the character in The Candidate. *Plastic. Teddy not only had all the answers; the human side came out. The warmth. The humor. Still, when the polls showed a close race, Romney must have seen a path to the presidency opening if he tamed the Lion of Liberalism. The path closed when the Lion roared, winning by 17 points. But it would open for Romney again in 2008 if he could show Republican primary voters that he'd brought conservative government to liberal Massachusetts.*

Dudley Square stepped on that story. Maybe Romney was afraid that his opponents would attack him for using the public sector to stimulate private investment—for believing that government is part of the solution when every conservative knows "government is the problem." Or that GOP voters would not reward him for siting a project in a black urban neighborhood. Or that DPH employees who didn't like working there would complain to Rush Limbaugh that they were pawns in a "liberal" social experiment. You guess at motives when reasons don't add up.

"The comeback of Dudley Square will be delayed for a while, but we'll get there," I said.

Though the city has fewer resources than the state, its eighteen thousand employees need places to work. But cities can't borrow to erect new buildings whenever a mayor wants. Capital budgeting has a rhythm dictating when cities can spend. Unfortunately, there was a long clock on major construction in Dudley Square.

We got there in stages. I asked the Boston Redevelopment Authority (BRA) for an analysis of all city services. The Police Department needed a replacement for its fortress-like station in Dudley Square. We commissioned the Boston firm Leers Weinzapfel Associates to construct a new $17.5 million B-2 district headquarters. Nearly half the workers on the job were minorities. The 35,000-square-foot building they put up received an environmental award for "green features" like daylighting and the city's first vegetative roof. The station's two hundred employees work in a healthy space.

The Ferdinand's eyesore remained, blighting the square. We decided to fill that space with the Boston School Department, relocating it from its 1909 building near City Hall. Putting school headquarters in Roxbury was fitting, since all but 10 percent of BPS students are minorities.

Five hundred school department employees are moving into a six-story $115 million building constructed behind the flatiron facade of Ferdinand's Blue Store. It is the tallest structure erected in Dudley Square in a century and, with 250,000 square feet overall and 25,000 square feet of retail space on the first floor, the biggest. The project occupies an entire block, and it will include wider sidewalks for outdoor cafés and space for a park next to the busy Dudley MBTA station.

This stylish new building, designed by an international team of architects, is an invitation to private investors to build in a district that can accommodate 2.4 million square feet of development. Some firms have already accepted the invitation. More will. The Dudley Square Vision Initiative opens a heady vista on a rising neighborhood at the geographic center of Boston.

"You're going to see a rejuvenation of this whole area," I said at the groundbreaking ceremony. "It's going to help people in the neighborhood stay put because there will be more jobs and economic opportunity. . . . We want people to raise their families there. That's what this is all about."

As I left office, a crane towered over Dudley Square. Cranes are familiar sights downtown. But this was the first anyone could remember in Roxbury. It was visible from far off, pointing up.

Chapter 2

The Struggle for the Schools

> That the common school should serve the Benefit of the Poor and the Rich; that the Children of all, partaking of equal Advantages and being placed upon an equal Footing, no Distinction might be made among them in the Schools on account of the different Circumstances of their Parents, but that the Capacity & natural Genius of each might be cultivated & improved for the future benefit of the whole Community.
>
> — *declaration of the Boston town meeting, 1784*

IT HAD NEVER been done before. No Boston mayor had ever publicly declared "judge me harshly" if he failed to fix the schools. I was the first one. I said it at my third State of the City address on January 17, 1996. I pointed my finger at the audience and at the thousands of Bostonians watching on television and charged them "to hold me accountable for what I have said tonight."

The setting, the auditorium of the Jeremiah E. Burke High School, shouted failure. The New England Association of Schools and Colleges measures schools by ten standards. The Burke had flunked eight.

The Burke's 940 students shared one guidance counselor. The science labs "imped[ed] instruction." In the civics textbooks used at the Burke, Martin Luther King Jr. was still alive; so was John F. Kennedy. The building was crumbling. It crumbled on me. On my first visit as mayor, a chunk of the auditorium ceiling fell on my shoulder.

The Burke was about to make history. Never before had a Massachusetts school lost its accreditation. That was a blow to the pride of the city that founded the public school. It was an embarrassment for me. It was a curse on the kids graduating from the Burke.

Kids like Diane Wolcott, who wanted to go to college so badly that she snuck into the perpetually closed library to research a history paper. Diane was a cheerleader. Leafing through a teen magazine she saw an announcement for a $10,000 scholarship for cheerleaders. Her hopes soared. Then she read the fine print: "You must be enrolled in an accredited high school."

The Burke was not alone. Six other Boston schools were on notice to shape up or share its disgrace.

"We're going to bring the schools back," I promised that night at the Burke. "In the most public of forums the mayor has staked his future on better schools," the *Boston Globe* commented. Statistics suggested the hard pull ahead:

- Forty-three of the system's 120 schools qualified for special state aid because their students did so poorly on state tests.
- In a recent test, juniors at Dorchester High had averaged 17 out of a possible 100 in reading, 18 in math.
- Nearly 40 percent of ninth-graders were dropping out before graduation.

I listed specific goals: a longer school day, computers in the classroom,* new standards in reading and math, and the rebuilding of most schools and the redesign of some as community learning centers. I gave myself six years to deliver. That would be the end of my second term. Of course, first I had to win a second term.

Commenting on my speech, John Nucci, former city councilor and School Committee member, outlined the "political risk" I was taking: "People don't vote for mayor on the performance of kids in the schools. It's crime, economic development, and just plain garbage pickup that drives the electorate in a mayor's race."

During the '93 campaign, my political consultants cited numbers making John's point. They urged me to campaign on crime, the first priority of 43 percent of voters, over education, picked by only 13 percent.

Fewer and fewer voters had a stake in the schools. The kids of the older whites whose property taxes paid for the minority kids in the system were long past school age. Nearly one in four young parents, like Robert Gittens, the first chair of my appointed school committee, sent their kids to parochial schools. Few of the "urban pioneers" moving into the South End, Jamaica Plain, and the Back Bay had kids of school age.

The dean of Harvard's Graduate School of Education saluted my "political courage" for tackling the schools, but I had not taken leave of my political senses. I knew that since World War II only one Bos-

* First the schools had to be wired for the Internet. Volunteers from the International Brotherhood of Electrical Workers laid seventy-one miles of cable to get the job done. They weren't the only volunteers. At an October 1997 event at the Curtis Guild School in Charlestown, Ted Kennedy, Bill Cosby, and I saluted the parents and teachers who donated ten thousand hours of personal time to bring computers to Boston's schools. A year later every school in the system was online.

ton mayor, James Michael Curley, had failed to win reelection, and he had been sentenced for mail fraud in his first term. I figured to clear that low bar.

Improving education was an odd mission to put at the heart of my mayoralty. Me, a C student who didn't go to college until my daughter went. When I graduated from the College of Public and Community Service at UMass Boston in 1988, journalists poked fun at me for receiving credit for "life experience." Yet that experience made me the right man to lead the struggle for the schools. "I'm the guy who came by education the hard way," I said at the Burke, "and that more than anything else qualifies me for this job."

It was a new job for a Boston mayor. For over a century, an elected school committee had run the schools — run them into the ground.

Under the elected committee, Boston operated two school systems, black and white, separate and unequal. It spent less on black students than on white, less for textbooks in black schools, and nearly a third less on health care for black kids. A state law passed in 1965 required racial balance in all public schools on the grounds that "racial imbalance represents a serious conflict with the American creed of equal opportunity." Yet thirty-five of Boston's schools had a black student enrollment of 65 to 95 percent. For a decade the School Committee took desperate steps, like counting Chinese students as white, to reduce the number of schools classified as racially imbalanced.

School Committee members won elections by resisting integration, not by improving the schools. As the quality of education deteriorated, they blamed the kids. "We have no inferior education in our schools," said one chairman. "What we have been getting is an inferior type of student." The schools weren't a priority for the Irish American pols who dominated the committee. They were in it for the jobs. They "took care of their own," as evidenced by the sixty-eight Sullivans, sixty-one Murphys, forty McCarthys, thirty O'Briens, and twenty-five Walshes on the School Department payroll in the 1960s.

As late as 1976 a panel of educators concluded: "Friends, neighbors, and relatives of School Committee members ask for and get special consideration for jobs. Who you know often counts more than what you know. . . . Job and employment questions pervade and poison the entire operation."

Turn-of-the-century reformers advocated elected school committees to "take the politics out of the schools." In Boston that worked, for a while. But after Maurice Tobin rose from the School Committee to mayor, governor, and then secretary of labor in Harry Truman's cabinet, members saw the committee as a ladder up in politics. Only a saint could resist pandering to the white electorate by promising to preserve their "neighborhood schools." But saints were rarer on the committee than Italians (two in seventy years).

Fanning the protest against busing, the court-mandated remedy for racial imbalance, committee chairs like Louise Day Hicks and John Kerrigan encouraged the belief that Judge Garrity's order could be resisted, though as lawyers they knew better. Their deceived supporters eventually turned them out of office.

The elected committee never recovered its prestige from the likes of Hicks — and especially Kerrigan, who, outside Judge Garrity's courtroom, once lampooned a black TV reporter by imitating a chimpanzee. Two mayors in a row, Kevin White and Ray Flynn, called for replacing this discredited elected body with one appointed by the mayor. But with support from whites protecting their jobs and from a black community defending the beachhead of its four seats on the thirteen-member committee, it survived into the early 1990s.

In 1991, when I was still on the City Council, I toured the shuttered Longfellow School in Roslindale with Brian Mooney of the *Boston Globe,* then running a five-part exposé of waste in the school budget. In the empty auditorium we found a grand piano. In the basement sat a $480,000 double boiler installed just weeks before the school closed in 1989. In a nearby room, eighty thousand sheets of paper rotted in puddles of water. Gesturing toward the paper, chalk, paints, and other supplies left behind, I said, "These are the things teachers tell us they buy out of their own pockets." How could the School Department just abandon them?

Court Street, shorthand for the city's school bureaucracy, had overspent eleven of its last thirteen budgets, boosting outlays 87 percent in a decade. In just four years, salaries for bus drivers had shot up 433 percent. Administrators were generous to themselves, too, taking half the department's fifty-two-car fleet home with them every night. Here, I told Mooney, was proof that "the dollar we give them isn't precious to them. The school budget is like a hole you can't get to the bottom of."

The elected school committee could not plug it. Instead, while planting their feet on the ladder of office, members argued over trivialities like whether the ad for a new superintendent should read "earned doctorate" or "earned doctorate preferred."

Ray Flynn had had enough. He held an advisory referendum on replacing the elected committee with a seven-member appointed one. The voters passed it, but by less than 1 percent. On that thread of support, in 1991 Flynn lobbied the state legislature to pass home-rule legislation creating an appointed school committee. The legislature attached a condition: The measure must pass a second referendum to be held in five years. The elected school committee was history.

Going out the door, in virtually their final act, the members signed a new school superintendent to a four-year contract. Flynn had wanted to appoint his own person. But he was stuck with the committee's choice. So was I.

Before the struggle for the schools could be joined, I had to clear three hurdles.

I had to settle the touchy issue of whether to renew Superintendent Lois Harrison-Jones's contract, which had nearly two years to run when I became mayor.

I had to find a superintendent who shared my sense of urgency about the schools. Boston, I feared, would turn into a city of the rich and the poor unless the middle class could be persuaded to trust their kids to the public schools. The 1990 census revealed a doubling in the number of residents in the upper income brackets since 1980 *and* an exodus of middle-income families of all races. Boston risked becoming Manhattan.

I wanted the Boston of the 90s and beyond to be a multiracial, multicultural version of my beloved Hyde Park of the 50s, a city of stable middle-class neighborhoods. Instead, it was increasingly a city of transients. Young couples moved in, stayed for five years, and when their kids reached first grade moved to the suburbs.

Finally, I had to persuade the voters not to restore the elected school committee, something polls showed 7 in 10 of them ready to do in a referendum scheduled for November 1996.

> It was torture every day to stay on top of my homework. I was sobbing every time I was doing math. The frustration was like a nightmare. My friend supported me by cheering me up in my desperate times. . . . I passed fourth grade, but I wasn't on my feet the next year. I got better, but still not enough to feel successful. I didn't pass fifth grade, but I was making progress

> in math. I no longer felt like an inept person. . . . At the end of fifth grade I got an award for the most improved in math. It felt like a dream. Obstacles are walls that can be broken.
>
> —*Every year, as part of the Max Warburg Courage Curriculum honoring an eleven-year-old Boston boy who died of leukemia in 1991, students submit essays on the meaning of courage. This passage is taken from an essay by Claudia Amador, a sixth-grader at the Patrick Lyndon Pilot School in 2007. It won a prize and was reprinted in the* Boston Globe.

In my 1994 inaugural address I noted that "for the first time since 1977 no African American holds a city-wide post." I pledged to "be especially responsive" to minority concerns. It was the least I could do. Blacks supported me in the election by nearly 4 to 1.

In 1990, when all but one of the white members of the School Committee voted to fire Boston's first African American superintendent of schools, Dr. Laval Wilson, the four black members walked out in protest. A prime minority concern was the future of Boston's only minority official, Wilson's successor, Superintendent Harrison-Jones.

She had a rough time of it in Boston. Ray Flynn sniped at her. The *Boston Globe* editorialized against her. She got off on the wrong foot with me.

It happened when I was still a city councilor. I was being interviewed by a television reporter in City Hall. Harrison-Jones was passing by. Hearing me mention a threatened strike by school bus drivers, she stopped in her tracks. Why are you asking *him* about *that?* she asked the reporter. He doesn't know anything about it . . . After that introduction, I bet she hoped that Jim Brett would beat me for mayor in the '93 election.

Little more than a month after the election, new tensions arose between Harrison-Jones and me.

On his way to a Dorchester Christmas party, Louis Brown, a fifteen-year-old straight-A student who dreamed of being the first black president, was killed in a gunfight between gangs. He was carrying a Secret Santa gift for a friend in Teens Against Gang Violence, the group holding the party, when he was shot in the head and dropped to the pavement, still holding the gift.

I drove out to Louis's house. Walking up the stairs, I remember thinking, *What can I say?* I rang the doorbell and Louis's mother, Tina Chéry, came down to see who it was. "I'm here to help," I said, and sat with her that night, listening to her stories about Louis. Consoling the loved ones of murdered children is part of a mayor's job in gun-saturated America.

The next day I attended Louis's funeral at St. Leo's Church. During the service, teenagers wearing black STOP GANG VIOLENCE sweatshirts stood in front of the wooden casket. In his sermon Bishop John Patrick Boles, Cardinal Bernard Law's representative, honored their cause when he spoke of Louis Brown as a "gentle young man who saw that opportunity could only be realized in a city of peace and hope."

I had to respond to Louis's murder and the contagion of gang violence. I proposed a twelve-month "boot camp" for fifty troubled (and troublemaking) teens recommended by school principals. I discussed it with the sheriff of Barnstable County on Cape Cod, who pioneered the state's first boot camp for adult offenders. The sheriff would run it, an in-the-woods experience to instill self-discipline. After boot camp, to reinforce the character they had found in themselves, the kids would be matched with long-term mentors. I had read a remark somewhere that D-Day was won in the CCC camps that FDR started during the Depression. Dispirited boys came out of the woods proud young men. I wanted that transformation for Boston kids tempted to seek self-esteem in gangs.

To me the boot camp was a matter of public safety. "It's an alternative program for these kids to get them back in the mainstream," I said. "It's better to do this than spend $50,000 . . . putting them in jail." Harrison-Jones saw it as an education issue — and met with me privately to complain that I had not cleared the idea with her. In the leak about our meeting that appeared in the press, "sources said she strongly register[ed] her disapproval."

Despite "the chilly winds that have blown between 26 Court Street and City Hall," I invited Superintendent Harrison-Jones to join my cabinet. The *Globe* applauded this "powerful statement of the mayor's commitment to educating the city's children." As I explained to reporters, this was "my way of reaching out. If we don't do something in the next two years, the schools are gone."

In a speech to business leaders in August 1994, I called the coming school term a "test year in which our commitment to carry out our agenda for change will be closely scrutinized." I had prodded the City Council to approve a $5 million increase in the school budget. A new teachers' contract offering greater flexibility in the classroom would be in place. Through the summer, more than one hundred teachers, administrators, and parents had drafted a new curriculum to raise student performance, partly through training parents to teach study skills at home. Five elementary schools, three middle schools, and two high schools were gearing up to try it. Their principals were reportedly displaying "high enthusiasm" for the experiment. All systems were go.

So I was disturbed to find out that because of "differences" between Court Street and the director of the Curriculum Renewal Team, the new curriculum would not be tried after all. There would be no test in the "test year." Remedial classes would not be ended.

Foreign language requirements would not be doubled. Algebra would not be introduced in the eighth grade. Parent activists would not be present in classrooms. The team director's reassignment just before the opening of school was what one school-watcher called "a terrible blow" to the project.

It was also a blow to a teacher whose proposal to require courses in African and African American history had been approved by the curriculum team. In words that stung me to read, he told a reporter: "The project was nothing more than a political statement to the public about making change. A lot of people were very excited about this project. It seemed a new era was developing."

My aides needed no prodding to leak the news that Harrison-Jones "has fallen out of favor with Menino." I expected that item to draw comment from African American politicians quick to defend Harrison-Jones. Mel King, a former state legislator who had run for mayor against Ray Flynn in 1983, went there: "We won't allow her to be lynched."

In the days leading up to the annual Martin Luther King Day breakfast held in the Marriott Copley Place ballroom, I braced myself for George Wallace comparisons.

David Nyhan recorded the moment: "The biggest needles of the day were reserved for Mayor Thomas Menino, who sat stoically through the 2½ hour extravaganza, whilst being on the receiving end of considerable advice that he rehire the Boston school superintendent, Lois Harrison-Jones, who sat at a floor table near Menino's end of the head table."

I was in a grim mood. Backstage, I'd exchanged hot words with Gareth Saunders, the city councilor from Roxbury. I don't take accusations of racism well.

I glanced at Governor Bill Weld sitting beside me, his face frozen in a "there but for the grace of God go I" mask. Weld's cuts in social services made him a target for this crowd. But not today; not with the bull's-eye painted on my back. *Thanks, pal,* I thought.

The speakers talked up Harrison-Jones's achievements — a falling dropout rate, four balanced budgets in a row, improved labor relations, and more. So why, they asked, did a School Committee member encourage her to apply for a teacher-training position in Virginia? Later that day, to a crowd of vocal supporters in a South End church, Harrison-Jones gave her answer.

She was "a victim of an unreachable standard of perfection." Boston was notorious for replacing school chiefs — eleven in twenty years — before they could show results: "I care too much about your children to roll over and play dead because someone says I should."

She was talking about me. Me implicitly in speaking of Boston's "peculiar fanaticism, an obsession with change for change's sake. [Officials] dart to and fro trying to find some . . . quick fix." And me directly: "People said there is need for the mayor to have his own person. That is political. The educational decision should have been based on whether there is movement. . . . The movement is there. . . . If Boston is to take its schools seriously, it has to get the politics out of the schools."

Substitute "accountability" for "politics" in that sentence and see if you still agree with it.

The crack about those wicked "politics" aside, Harrison-Jones made a strong case for patience. For giving the next superintendent time to follow through. She was right: There was no quick fix. School reform was steady work. Beneath her swipes at me, she was passing along earned wisdom.

Two days after the Martin Luther King Day breakfast, I was relieved to read in the *Globe* that "Boston School Superintendent Lois Harrison-Jones said yesterday that she does not intend to wage a public fight to stay on after her contract expires in June, a move that appeared to defuse a budding confrontation with Mayor Menino over her future."

In February the School Committee voted against extending Harrison-Jones's contract for an additional year. Committee chair Felix Arroyo said a lame-duck superintendent could not push through the changes the system needed.

I happened to be in Florida, which raised eyebrows. That wily Menino! "He walks away from this whistling like a Charlie Chaplin character," said Mike McCormack, a former colleague on the City Council. "She has been surgically removed without his hand being seen on the knife." If only I were that deft.

It's true I hated letting people go. I know what losing a job means when you have a mortgage and kids. But my vacation was scheduled in advance of the School Committee's vote on Dr. Harrison-Jones. And it was no secret that, in major matters, the committee acted for me.

From Florida I issued a statement: "I deeply appreciate all the superintendent has done for the children and families of Boston. She has demonstrated complete and total commitment and caring."

At the Martin Luther King Day breakfast Harrison-Jones received a standing ovation. She deserved it.

> In my case, courage meant to tell my friends about a religion that they knew little about.
>
> On a September day in 2001 as I was walking home, I felt sadness in the air. I walked inside my house and saw my whole family glued to the news on TV. My mom walked toward me and said, "Ya, Allah (Oh, God)" and gave me a hug. . . .

> I showed courage by going to school and telling every student and teacher who may think of me as "different" because I wear a scarf on my head that I am a Muslim, not a terrorist.
>
> —*from a prizewinning 2005 essay in the Max Warburg Courage Curriculum by Shukri Abdillahi, then a sixth-grader at the James P. Timilty Middle School*

"WANTED: Boston School Superintendent. Brainless, featureless doormat wanted to revive dead school system. Short-term position. Must be willing to be buffeted about unmercifully by clueless pols." Written by a columnist close to the African American community, that ad spoofed a perception I had to change. And do it before the November referendum on the School Committee.

My only course was to hire an outstanding new superintendent. Someone universally respected in education circles. Someone whose reputation for independence signaled that he or she would not be buffeted about by a "clueless pol" (me). Someone who would not stay in Boston if the voters brought back the old committee.

A distinguished search committee began vetting candidates who applied for the job, and I relied on their professional judgment. Then Senator Ted Kennedy called me to recommend a candidate who had not applied.

When Ted spoke, I listened. I loved the guy. I miss him. A sad moment in my life came in August 2009, when Angela and I stood in front of City Hall to watch Ted's funeral procession as the Faneuil Hall bell tolled forty-seven times, once for each year Ted served in the Senate.

Once we were both scheduled to speak at the opening of a photonics lab at Boston University. Ted leaned over to me prior to the press conference:

TED: What's photonics?

ME: How would I know? You got the grant.

TED: What are you going to say?

ME: Whatever *you* say, pal. I'm not going to deviate from your script.

Boston had no warmer friend in Washington than Teddy Kennedy. In 1994, when he was in trouble running for reelection in a Republican year, Boston had his back. The race will be won in the city, I told my people. Get out the vote for Ted Kennedy! Late in the campaign, a senior member of my administration informed me that he was voting for Ted's opponent, Mitt Romney. He could have hit me with a mallet. You work for Boston's mayor, I shouted, yet you won't vote for Boston's senator? I had appointed this guy? I ordered him to be at one of Boston's busiest traffic circles at seven the next morning. A KENNEDY FOR SENATE sign would be waiting for him. I expected him to stand out on that rotary holding that sign all day, and told him I'd drive by to check. But I didn't say when.

Ted's candidate was Assistant Secretary of Education Thomas Payzant. Ted's Education and Labor Committee had approved Payzant's appointment in the Clinton administration. Payzant's job was to promote school change. It seemed too good to be true.

Tom was a local boy, from nearby Quincy, educated at Williams College and at Harvard's Graduate School of Education, whose first teaching job was in suburban Belmont. A decade later, at age thirty-two, he was heading the Eugene, Oregon, school system. He stepped on toes there, transferring politically connected principals who were not doing their jobs. He moved on to Oklahoma City, where he mobilized parents to get involved in the schools. In San Diego, his last stop before Washington, he won both praise and criticism for his focus on raising student test scores.

I called Payzant to encourage him to apply. He sounded up for it. We were both scheduled to be in New York on the same day. So we met for lunch at the Carnegie Deli. I didn't hire by résumé. I always loved that part, "references will be furnished upon request." Who ever gave a bad reference? You give your mother-in-law, your wife, your three kids. I went more by my gut. I didn't interview candidates for jobs. I met them. We talked. Usually about everything other than the job — the kids, where they lived, their other interests. When we didn't click, it was like you threw a ball and no one was there to catch it. Tom Payzant caught it. One of my aides sat with us until we tucked into our corned beef sandwiches. When he came back an hour or so later, we were talking like old friends.

Payzant didn't oversell the Payzant cure for the schools. Progress would be slow. He promised setbacks. Guaranteed mistakes. But he also spoke of cooperation as a force for change. Through joint effort and open communication, the teachers and staff of the Boston Public Schools would get there . . . Where? A better education for the kids. And his voice warmed when he mentioned the kids. Sure, he had a Harvard Ph.D. But he wouldn't have got the job without that. Following protocol for federal officials, he paid for his own lunch. A small sign of integrity not lost on me.

An education reporter asked Payzant something many in Boston were curious about: Why "as a federal official who had once headed a district [San Diego] twice the size of Boston" did he want to come here? "There seems to be an unusual opportunity in Boston right now," he replied, with the accountable mayor, the appointed school committee, and the professional superintendent all on the same team, all pulling in the same direction. "It is rare that this happens in a major city."

Boston's next superintendent, Payzant thought, faced twin challenges: convincing the public that "change and excellence" are "doable" *and* that change takes time. Those challenges defined the ten-year struggle for the schools.

On one side, school reform had to fight "the soft bigotry of low expectations," former President George W. Bush's phrase for the belief that "those kids can't hack it"—that the schools can't compensate for the injuries inflicted by poverty and racial isolation. "You can't make gold out of straw," said one teacher, speaking anonymously to a reporter. "We are asked to do so much, be everything, everybody. You need dedicated parents. Kids' friends are being shot and then they come to school. Do you want to try to teach them?"

Well-meaning minority voices called Payzant's fixation on raising scores unfair. Why make poor city kids take tests with built-in upper-middle-class bias? Lower the bar. Adjust the scale. Shield city kids, at least temporarily, from discovering how far behind suburban kids they are.

If one side was resigned to the status quo or protective of it, the other demanded change yesterday. Why aren't scores rising faster? Why, Mr. Mayor, keep Payzant on year after year when he has produced so few "deliverables"? Why *can't* those kids hack it?

Payzant took charge at Court Street on October 1, 1995. A December poll found voters "overwhelmingly" in favor of restoring the elected school committee in the referendum less than a year away.

The polls consistently predicted I was on the wrong side of "Question No. 2." Friends advised me: Walk away from a lost cause. The voters want an elected committee. Don't stand in their way. But the big wheel of politics was turning my way. Nineteen ninety-six was a presidential election year. Turnout was expected to be double what it was for the first referendum on the School Committee held during the 1989 City Council elections. Running as an incumbent, Bill Clinton would pull out the vote in neighborhoods that took a pass on city elections — the South End, Mission Hill, the Back Bay, Beacon Hill. Their liberal "good government" voters would respond to my case that the elected committee had been a hive of "shameless grandstanding, rampant patronage, and dirty politics."

On the other side, champions of the elected committee advanced a superficially appealing populist counterargument: Let the voters decide. Only elites who don't trust "the people" could be against democratic control of the schools. I bridled at that charge. I trusted the people to hold the mayor accountable for the schools. What was undemocratic about that?

Not so fast, retorted opponents like State Senator Dianne Wilkerson, who represented a minority district: "How do you get accountability for the schools? You can't expect it when it depends on one man who's in charge of everything in the city." Unlike a school committee facing the voters every two years, a busy mayor serving four years would lose track of the schools.

Another black official warned minority voters that if they voted no, the Old South would rise again . . . in Boston. The white mayor, the white members of the appointed school committee, and the white superintendent overseeing the mostly minority kids in the Boston schools would succumb to a "plantation mentality." I was lucky the circumstances didn't invite "lynching."

The Question 2 referendum was *the* critical vote of my two decades in office. I took it so seriously that I *sought* debates with "yes" supporters. In a televised duel held on the marble steps of the altar at Trinity Church, my opponent, City Councilor Mickey Roache, scored when he pointed out that the Burke, a symbol of failure, lost its accreditation under *my* appointed committee. It was the kind of moment your handlers try to smooth over: "Don't worry, Mayor. Nobody watched the thing. *Monday Night Football* was on"—even if it was Wednesday.

We conducted two campaigns. One of public education. The other of political mobilization.

In the months ahead of the vote, we brought together different constituencies to hear our case. Several evenings a week, my education adviser Martha Pierce and I left City Hall and went to a nearby campaign office. There we spoke to groups of parents, teachers, principals, university presidents, and other interested parties. We also took our show on the road, to community newspapers, to senior centers, to school auditoriums, to living rooms.

The issue did not break down neatly on racial lines. Though polls in white neighborhoods indicated strong opposition to the appointed committee, some of the stiffest resistance came from minority parents. They hated to lose those four members of the old School Committee, the only black elected officials in city history. But those black members were outnumbered by conservative whites. Our appointed committee, by contrast, was majority minority. That's why the Urban League supported us, and why a former head of the Boston NAACP had agreed to run the "no" campaign.

Another common objection to the appointed committee was that it gave me too much power. I could stack the committee with political hacks.

Our pushback was to remind people of the checks and balances written into the enabling legislation passed in 1991. It vested the power to nominate School Committee members in a board of prestigious figures from education, business, and nonprofits. The board had thirteen members; nine were chosen by the governor and a committee of the legislature, only four by the mayor. I couldn't pack the School Committee with hacks even if I wanted to.

But that was the last thing I wanted. With feeling in my voice, I promised parents, "I'm in this fight for your kids, not my power."

It helped our side that Question 2 read like it had begun life in a foreign language, with a "no" vote signifying yes to the appointed committee. How could the city election department let that happen?

It helped that the "Vault," a group of Boston employers alive to appeals from the same City Hall that assessed their property, kicked in $600,000 to finance TV ads, 235 times what the "yes" folks managed to raise. And although I want big money out of politics, I admit it helped that, on referendum questions, corporations can contribute directly and without limit to favored causes.

On Labor Day we mounted a full-court press, flooding the city with signs, holding rallies, gaining endorsements. Counting the Timilty-White fights, this was my ninth Boston election. I knew how winning campaigns felt. This one didn't feel right. By early October, the post–Labor Day momentum was draining away. "No" needed help.

I asked my friend Bob "Skinner" Donahue, with twenty-five years of experience running national, state, and local campaigns, to build a parallel field organization. Suddenly bumper stickers were everywhere. Calls from phone banks interrupted suppers. Signs sprouted on lawns.

The appearance of momentum was back. The reality would follow. That's what campaigns do.

I devoted nearly all my time to the campaign, working the phones to raise money, micromanaging tactics, motivating the troops, taking my case to the voters in neighborhood open houses. In a key battleground, Ward 20 in West Roxbury, I walked door-to-door, and on election night showed up to press the flesh at two precincts.

A poll conducted in the last week of the campaign found 44 percent for the appointed committee, 25 percent for the elected committee. But 22 percent were undecided. How would they tip?

On Election Day, Angela visited precincts all over the city. Things seemed to be going our way. "As people came to the polls, they winked, they patted me on the shoulder, they said great things," she told me. That night, in the Eagle Room off my fifth-floor office, the "no" gang waited for the results to come in.

Donahue had compiled a list of fifty swing districts. Ward 8, Precinct 6, in Roxbury was the first to report. In 1989 it had voted for an appointed committee by 5 percent; now by 23 percent. Next came Ward 1, Precinct 12, in Orient Heights, East Boston. Against an appointed committee in '89, now it was for, 440 to 183.

I worry till the polls close. You can fall for your own campaign. Mistake campaign-generated enthusiasm for the real thing. Over Question 2, I had been on edge for weeks. As a City Hall reporter noted, "Question No. 2 is Obsession No. 1 with the mayor." Neil Sullivan, director of the Private Industry Council and an adviser to me on the referendum, agreed: "It's become such a cause for him. . . . It's as if this intensity for schools has become part of his political identity." So much was at stake.

The eyes of the education world were on Boston. "There's more hope around the Boston Public Schools than there has been in the 15 to 20 years I've been around," observed Jerry Murphy from Harvard's Graduate School of Education. "You have to hope Payzant and Menino can do it." Along with Chicago, Boston was a pioneer in mayor-driven school change. Twenty-first-century mayors and educators could learn from our successes and failures. "If it can work here, it can work anywhere," said Murphy.

The eyes of Boston's politicians were on me. The vote would be read as a verdict on my administration. If my side lost, I'd draw a strong opponent in the upcoming mayoral election.

But now, as Skinner's bellwether wards began to fall our way, the tension eased. I punched the air with my fists, squeezed Skinner's shoulders, and whooped in victory. Just then Tom Payzant walked in to congratulate me. Ed Jesser, my longtime friend and political adviser, grabbed Payzant and yelled, "OK, you can stay in town, kid."

By 3 to 1, the people had spoken. The kid could stay in town.

> I was born in Quito, Ecuador. . . . At the Josiah Quincy Upper School, kids made fun of me because I was adopted and had white parents. . . . I sometimes felt like punching them, but as Martin Luther King said, "Learn to love your enemies." Therefore I was kind and gentle. . . . Courage means to ignore the people who bother you and to love the ones you love. . . . The parents who adopted me are the ones I love a lot.
>
> —*Jefferson Payne, sixth-grader at the Josiah Quincy School in 2007*

A friend remarked that changing the Boston schools was like "turning the *Titanic* around in a bathtub." Performing that feat was now the job of the new captain.

When Tom Payzant cautioned, "It could be years before the numbers turn around," I groaned. How long should the kids have to wait for the schools they deserved? And I didn't have "years." I had until 2001, when I invited voters to "judge me harshly" if scores weren't up.

Payzant set his course to 2003, when, for the first time, all high school seniors in Massachusetts were scheduled to take a graduation exam, the capstone of the Massachusetts Comprehensive Assessment System (MCAS). In the landmark Education Reform Act of 1993, the state legislature committed hundreds of millions in state aid to improve local schools. By the late 90s, cities and towns had been spending the money for years. MCAS would measure how well. Seniors who failed to pass the tenth-grade standard would not receive diplomas. Failing schools would be exposed. Jobs would be on the line. The reckoning would come in a seventeen-hour test spread over three days.

Payzant geared everything to MCAS. "All our efforts in Boston are now focused on this challenge," he wrote in an op-ed column. "We are undertaking massive professional development in all our schools for teachers and administrators. We are providing up to 12 months of intensive instruction and extra supports — at a cost of more than $20 million — for students behind grade level in grades 3, 6, and 9. We are aligning our curricula to the state tests. We are holding ourselves accountable for results."

His first year on the job, Payzant substituted the more rigorous "Stanford 9" for the test taken in most urban school systems. The Stanford revealed that without dramatic progress, one-half of seventh-graders would not graduate from high school. "A tough reality check," Payzant called the test. A Roxbury girl called it "horrible."

For some students, high-stakes tests didn't motivate them to try harder but discouraged them from trying, period. Kids need success to succeed. But how would they know they had succeeded if they didn't pass a test? I got that. Still, no great shakes at test taking myself, testing's casualties weighed on my conscience.

Payzant's plan was comprehensive:

- Since every minute of teaching time counted in the race against MCAS, disruptive middle school students, whose acting out cost their classmates 20 percent of their learning time, would be sent to a school set up to handle them.

- With the typical Boston high school student absent twenty-eight days a year, Payzant moved to curtail truancy. Kids couldn't afford to lose the class time.
- Through social promotion, kids had been failing upward. MCAS ended social promotion. But holding kids back encouraged them to drop out. Threading that policy needle, Payzant replaced social promotion with mandatory summer school. Fifty percent of failing students in grades 3, 5, and 7 attended one summer, all eighth-graders the next.
- Under the "2 to 6" initiative, which I started before Payzant came aboard, more schools were staying open longer for test prep and other activities.

Following a Menino best practice, Payzant frequently got away from Court Street, visiting at least two of the city's 127 schools every week, and shaking hands with teachers, students, parents, and custodians. These were friendly visits. They were also unannounced. "We have got to keep the pressure on," Payzant said, as the months marched toward May 2003.

> I was about 2 when my brother and I went to live with my father. My father was still in high school. My mother dropped us off at my father's house; I didn't see her again for a long time. . . . My father could have sent us both to a foster home . . . but instead he asked my grandparents to help him raise us. My father . . . never quit trying to make his life better for him and for us. For example, he finished high school and went to college. He is now a registered nurse at Brigham and Women's Hospital. . . . My father is always an inspiration, and when I am feeling down I go to him and he encourages me to do my best. My father was 18 and took on the responsibility of raising two

> children when he was a child himself. . . . Courage is accepting responsibility for one's actions, in spite of the obstacles, and reaching for the stars!
>
> —*Darianna Santana, sixth-grader at the Solomon Lewenberg Middle School in 2009*

At the Burke, I vowed to make that failing school the "pride of Boston." Payzant's "incremental progress" toward MCAS is a two-yards-and-a-cloud-of-dust story. The Burke's story is more dramatic, and more heartbreaking. It highlights the fragility of progress in urban education.

In the weeks surrounding my speech, if you had looked through the *Globe*'s obituary pages, you would have seen photographs of women who graduated from the Burke in the 30s, 40s, and 50s. A number had won scholarships to Radcliffe, Wellesley, Smith, and Barnard. A few had pursued graduate study at Oxford or the Sorbonne. Wives and mothers and grandmothers, they had also been writers and scientists and educators. Named for a former school superintendent who died in 1931, and opened three years later, the Burke was their launching pad, an Art Deco palace of cultural enrichment for the mainly Jewish and Irish Catholic girls of Dorchester.

Times change. By the late 1960s, Grove Hall, the Burke's once-safe neighborhood, was gang-ridden. The school went coed in 1972, and like all of Boston's high schools in the 70s it was rocked by busing.

In 1982, when Albert Holland, an assistant headmaster at South Boston High in the eye of the busing storm, was appointed the Burke's fourth headmaster in three years, he found a school in chaos. The bathrooms were locked to prevent students from fighting or sexually assaulting one another inside. The halls reeked of human waste. Teachers locked themselves in their classrooms.

One of Holland's first acts was to chain the front doors to keep out gangs.

"Nobody cared about the Burke," Holland said later. "It was a dumping ground for all the have-nots."

Supported by Superintendent Robert R. Spillane, Holland set out to bring back the Burke. With an infusion of cash from Court Street, he hired more staff, cleaned and painted the rooms and halls, and invited twenty social service agencies — engaged in everything from pregnancy counseling to dress-for-success coaching — to operate in the school. Importantly, he lowered the Burke's enrollment.

More money, more staff, more services, fewer kids: the formula for school success. It worked. By 1990, national magazines were hailing the Burke as one of the country's best public schools. Seventy percent of its graduates went to college. "We had kids going to Cornell, Bates, Michigan, Boston College," Holland recalled. "We even had a dream of restoring Latin."

Then the dream lost its subsidy. A city budget crunch in the recession of the early 90s cost the Burke its supplemental funding. Staff were laid off. Enrollment sharply increased. The formula for school failure.

Holland left in 1993. It was a promotion, to assistant superintendent. But he was also shaken: A student stabbed during a lunch period had nearly bled out in his arms. He recalled praying, "My God, don't let this child die." The child lived. The Burke spiraled down.

Inspectors from the New England Association of Schools and Colleges, weighing whether to suspend the Burke's accreditation, discovered that the school had no drinking water. Holland told Mayor Flynn that "if this was a white school in a white neighborhood, this [deterioration] would not be tolerated."

Steve Leonard, the new headmaster, recalled the day *he* first walked into the Burke: "There was smoke in the corridors, the coke machine was cracked and its fluorescent lights were flashing like a penny arcade. [T]eachers would stand in the hallways grabbing kids they thought were salvageable and slam the doors."

In 1996 I committed to a five-year plan to bring back the Burke . . . again. The Burke would get $5 million more a year (almost double the 1995 total) to hire more teachers and counselors and renovate the building. Enrollment was cut. Staff increased. Going forward, the maximum teacher-student ratio at the Burke would be 1 to 24, compared to 1 to 33 at other city high schools.

By 1998, under the dynamic Leonard, the Burke had regained its accreditation. That year it enrolled 671 students: 591 were black, 42 Hispanic, 20 Asian, 16 white, and 2 Native American. Twenty-four percent were bilingual. Nineteen percent were special needs—kids with learning disabilities and behavioral problems, some serious.

Leonard had picked his own staff: teachers and counselors who went the extra mile. A girl who could not live with her drug-addicted mother moved in with her ailing grandmother, who died, leaving the girl homeless. Caring staff found her a place to live with a friend of the Burke. "They've done this for a lot of other kids, at least seven seniors I know of," the girl told a reporter.

On the academic side, Leonard wanted the Burke's students to take their place in the knowledge society. For kids who blew off higher education ("Truman didn't go to college"), there'd be no strong-back, high-wage manufacturing jobs at a Westinghouse plant in twenty-first-century Boston. What they earned would depend on what they learned at the Burke and beyond. "We just convinced them they couldn't graduate until they applied to college," Leonard said. "We were bluffing. But it worked."

By 2001, the Burke was one of three high schools nationwide recognized by the College Board for sending all of its eligible seniors to two- or four-year colleges. All 154. Everybody but the fourteen in jail and the four undocumented immigrants barred from college by their status. "Now we have proof to show people what we can do," said one young graduate on her way to a summer session at Phillips Exeter Academy before enrolling at the University of New Hampshire.

The Burke was back! And the five-year time limit on the extra resources I had steered to the Burke since 1996 was up.

> Courage is simply living today in this society. There are too many crazy people that can hurt you. . . . I think it takes a lot of courage just to get up every morning and go outside your door and go to school. . . . It takes a lot of courage to go to the store not knowing what may happen to you while you are just trying to do an errand for your parents.
>
> —*Jemaro Reheem Strictland, sixth-grader at the Woodrow Wilson School in Dorchester in 1994*

In 2001, an election year, I had run out of time.

I had no opponent in 1997, a twentieth-century first. The *Globe* gave me a dishwater endorsement: "He is essentially a sound, second-tier mayor who had the good fortune to ride the development, investment and job growth crests of a strong national economy during his first term." Luckily "[Menino] had the good sense to make the most of them." I quoted the bad so I could quote the good: "No mayor in America . . . has gone further in accepting personal accountability for the quality of public education."

My opponent in 2001, City Councilor Peggy Davis-Mullen of South Boston, had nerve running. She was facing allegations that she had underreported her income on her 2000 taxes; failed to file her tax returns for 1998 and 1999; made false statements on two applications to the Massachusetts Bar; hired a chief of staff who ran afoul of the residency requirement for city employees; and bypassed a waiting list to get her twin sons into a desirable pilot school program. These revelations broke over her campaign in less than two weeks. The few who contribute to candidates in city elections gave nothing to her. And the preliminary election fell two weeks after the 9/11 terrorist attacks on New York and the Pentagon created a local media blackout on the campaign. Mike McCormack, the former city councilor, didn't overstate my chances when he said, "I don't see anything that would threaten the mayor, absent being taken by aliens."

Davis-Mullen made the schools an issue, urging voters to hold me to my bold words. "This is the same mayor who said judge me and judge me harshly if I haven't made progress on education in 2001, and he most emphatically has not," she charged. "The kids who took the MCAS last year, you have 84% failing the math portion. . . . How many headmasters have been replaced? I don't see any real accountability. . . . I would make a very strong commitment to making sure kindergarten for 4-year-olds exists. I would like to see us reduce class size."

My record got a more mixed assessment from two education writers. On the one hand, test scores had "inched up," the city had spent millions "repairing decrepit schools," and seniors were attending college "at higher rates than six years ago and above the national average." On the other, the dropout rate was "stagnant," the gap in test scores between the races was as wide as ever, and "reported crimes on school grounds" were rising, including thirty-eight assaults on teachers in one school term. Overall these beat reporters judged me harshly: "Mayor Thomas M. Menino's record is one of painstaking change delivered in small steps, not the radical restructuring many had hoped for."

I could quibble with that. But always believe an objective source over a politician. I do.

School chiefs in big cities don't last more than two or three years. Parents have no patience with change. Mayors and school boards are reluctant to ask them to wait. Their kids are in school now. They want results now. Blame for the slow pace of improvement and for the shakiness of progress in resource-limited school systems that must rob Peter to pay Paul — that blame falls on the superintendent of schools.

I took the heat for my superintendents. Tom Payzant stayed eleven years; Carol Johnson, his successor, six. They could do the steady work of change shielded from the politics of impatience.

Payzant cleared the 2003 hurdle. Boston's kids came through. They worked hard. It paid off. In 1998, only 35 percent of Boston fourth-graders passed the MCAS for the lower grades. In 2005, 60 percent of fourth-graders and 75 percent of tenth-graders passed. And the 25 percent who didn't had two more years to meet their graduation requirements. In 2006, the Broad Foundation named the Boston Public Schools the best city system in the country. A report for the Rennie Center for Education Research and Policy described Payzant's achievement this way: "Suddenly education advocates were demanding to know why so few students were scoring in the proficient and advanced categories. Payzant had transformed the system from one where failure was assumed to one where merely passing was not good enough."

Until her husband's illness forced her retirement, Carol Johnson built on Tom Payzant's foundation. She breathed human warmth into the statistical language of education. If I'm supposed to have met half of Boston's residents, Carol must have hugged half of Boston's sixty thousand students. Besides emotion, she brought values and vision to the cause. "Public education can transform lives and end intergenerational poverty," she wrote. "The education of our children is a moral endeavor so central to our purpose that, should we fail, our very existence will be in peril."

Her life story would make an uplifting movie. Her mother, a rural Tennessee schoolteacher, spent her summer vacations pursuing graduate study at the University of Michigan. Her father ran a barber shop and billiards parlor in Brownsville, sixty miles northeast of Memphis. It was the segregated South, and Carol and her eight siblings learned early what separate and unequal meant. The white schools offered kindergarten, but the black kids had to wait until first grade to enter the black schools. The white schools got the latest textbooks; the black schools, hand-me-down old ones from the white schools. "People didn't dwell on that," Johnson reflected decades later. Discrimination "wasn't an excuse not to read, not to write, not to perform."

Carol's parents met at Fisk University; so did Carol and her husband, Matthew. Both became teachers. Carol taught third grade in the Washington, D.C., schools, paying for paper and crayons out of her own pocket. Veteran teachers told her not to smile until November. History doesn't record how long she made it. My bet is the second day of school.

Minneapolis was where she first made her name as a school leader. The *Star Tribune* dubbed her the "superintendent with a halo" for her calming influence on a troubled system. Memphis wooed her away. For her work *there* she was named Superintendent of the Year by the Tennessee Parent-Teacher Association. Boston wooed her away from Memphis.

Our search committee put her name at the top of the list. The School Committee chair, Elizabeth Reilinger, seconded their recommendation. Reilinger and I and another committee member,

Reverend Gregory Groover, met with her in Memphis. "They spent many hours being persistent and very persuasive," she said. Being obnoxious was probably more like it.

The Memphis School Board greeted the news with this statement: "Boston saw we had a jewel, and they're taking it away from us." Phil Bredesen, the governor of Tennessee, called her: "I told her congratulations — and that I might forgive her in the next few years." She'd launched a media campaign with the theme "Every Child, Every Day, College Bound." At a farewell ceremony held in a school auditorium, Carol kept her composure until a fourth-grader reached this point in his speech: "I am a member of the graduating class of 2015. Until then, we will remain College Bound." Then tears streaked her cheeks, and she wrapped the boy in a hug.

I witnessed the local sorrow. As I told reporters, "I never saw a city rally and work so hard to keep a superintendent of schools." I was afraid she'd respond to pleas to run for mayor of Memphis.

"I expect to hit the ground listening," she said about her new job. She heard an earful. In Memphis she could fire failing school principals. She couldn't do that in Boston, the teachers' union told her. She wanted teachers to stay in school at least an hour longer after the bell rang. No, the union said, not unless teachers received higher pay. That's not possible, *I* told her. Tax revenues had fallen in the slowing economy, and $33 million had to be cut from the school budget.

Some ideas about raising student achievement await proof. Not the longer school day. Consider the evidence from Lawrence, among the poorest cities in Massachusetts. Several years ago the state appointed a receiver to run its failing schools, vesting him with the power to bypass union work rules. The school week was extended seven hours. Lawrence kids receive an extra hour of small-group tutoring four days a week and two and a half hours of "enrichment"—yoga, theater, athletics, cooking—on Fridays. One K–8 school rose from Level 3 on the MCAS to Level 1 in a single year. What changed? According to the principal, "Students have more time for learning than ever before." The longer day "makes the impossible possible."

Boston has one of the shortest school days in the country, an hour shorter than in cities like Charlotte, Nashville, and Austin. I wanted a longer school day to make the impossible possible for Boston's kids, but the union put the kids second. The voters want the kids put first. They are fed up with the conflict between teachers' rights to collective bargaining and students' rights to a first-class education. (In fairness, some of the things the union demands for teachers—smaller classes, up-to-date textbooks, healthy school buildings—also benefit their students.) They are fed up with a 255-page Boston Teachers Union contract that bars flexibility in hiring, permits burned-out teachers with seniority to "bump" better teachers out of their jobs, and protects teachers who aren't performing.

Public willingness to pay for the public schools is eroding. This trend can only hurt teachers' pocketbooks. That is the handwriting on the wall. Will union leaders read it before even Democratic politicians take up the cry to privatize education?

The new superintendent favored charter schools. I was cool to them.

Under state law, children attending charters take with them a slice of the state aid sent to their local school districts. I persuaded the City Council to hold Boston's schools harmless by covering that loss. In 2002, for students attending the city's ten charter schools, it came to $14 million. A decade later, the city's public schools lost over $80 million in state aid to two dozen charters.

My objection to charters goes deeper than money. Charters aren't inclusive. They don't take everybody. Boston's public schools take everybody.

They take the kids—from Iraq, from Afghanistan, from Somalia—who can't speak English. The kids with learning disabilities. The kids who get their only good meal at school. The kids who act out. These kids need every break. Their schools need every dime. But charters drain money and, as important, motivated students from them.

Forget practice; that's wrong in theory. Charter schools are not compatible with the ideal of the common school handed down by the Boston town meeting of 1784—"that the Children of all, partaking of equal Advantages and being placed upon an equal Footing, no Distinction might be made among them in the Schools." Notice those big words: "all" children, "equal" advantages. Not the few gaining at the expense of the many.

However, two elections persuaded me to give ground on charters. The first was the 2008 presidential election. The new Obama administration proposed to divide $4 billion among states that could demonstrate "innovation in education," code for charter schools. The second was the 2009 Boston mayoral election campaign. When two candidates running against me gained traction by calling for more charters, I recognized that the voters wanted change.

Governor Deval Patrick was pushing a bill to considerably increase the number of charter schools in the lowest-performing districts. It empowered the state's Board of Education to remove bad teachers, change curriculums, and extend the school day. I was for the reforms but against the charters. So I filed a bill to create charters that met my concerns over fairness. Local school committees would control these "in-district" charters. Unlike traditional charters, they would not drain state money from the regular public schools and they would take everybody. The governor agreed to splice my bill with his.

The teachers' union opposed in-district charters because they would operate free of collective bargaining constraints, and it had paid to elect many state legislators. It was time to remind these Democrats to put kids first. Especially after the House, caving to the union, dropped the in-district charters passed by the Senate. I was in a rehabilitation hospital with a bum leg. But that didn't stop me from haranguing members over the phone. I put on my hot-under-the-collar act. Hanging up on one rep, I told my press secretary Dot Joyce, "I'll bet I gave *him* brown pants!"

My lobbying helped sway the House to restore in-district charters. But the first education reform bill in sixteen years passed because as much as $300 million in federal aid was at risk if it didn't.

The *Globe* rated inclusion of the in-district charters "a major victory . . . at the expense of the teachers union . . . for Mayor Thomas M. Menino."

I wanted to run an experiment. Could the longer school day and other reforms in the law convert a failing school into a successful one? The testing ground was the Patrick F. Gavin Middle School in South Boston, a last resort for students who'd been unable to get into the schools of their choice. With the same students, could a new in-district charter show big gains?

To make the experiment work, we turned to Scott Given, a thirty-two-year-old graduate of the Harvard Business School with a track record in education. His nonprofit, Unlocking Potential, had done an excellent job running a charter school in East Boston. New Haven was courting him. I asked him to stay in Boston and transform the Gavin. He agreed, renaming the school UP Academy. That was the right direction.

UP Academy opened in August 2010. In September, I met an academy teacher at a Red Sox game. She said the first weeks had been rough, but the kids were taking to the new curriculum and their new teachers. See for yourself, she said, and invited me to sit in on a class.

I asked her seventh-graders how many were at the Gavin in 2009. They all raised their hands. I asked a sixth-grade class. No hands were raised. I couldn't hide my disappointment. The whole idea was to see what UP could do with the Gavin's students. Then Martha Pierce reminded me that UP was a middle school, which admitted a new sixth-grade class every year, and my smile returned.

Scott Given promised quick results. And did he ever deliver! On the 2010 MCAS exams, 32 percent of the Gavin's students were ranked proficient in English and just 23 percent in math. A year later, at UP Academy, 54 percent scored proficient in English and 48 percent in math. The math scores had grown more than at any other school in the state.

UP Academy is succeeding not because it requires students to wear black shirts and khaki pants. Not because it sheds challenging kids: Its 2012 "withdrawal rate" of 19 percent was below the district average of 22 percent and the Gavin's historical average of 25 percent. And not because Scott Given is a turnaround genius. UP Academy's teachers and staff have succeeded where the Gavin's failed partly because UP has fifteen more teachers than the Gavin, and this allows them to collaborate on lesson plans and teaching strategies for over an hour a day. But the biggest reason UP has unlocked the potential of students floundering at the Gavin is that the school day is ninety minutes longer than the regular schools' six and a half hours. There is extra time for classes and enrichment activities, and at the end of every day, every student receives an hour of tutoring. That's how UP Academy makes the impossible possible. Children in all Boston's schools could flourish like the UP students. All that stands in the way is the Boston Teachers Union's resistance to a longer school day.

Over Carol Johnson's six years at Court Street, the good numbers went up. Fifty-five percent of tenth-graders passed the MCAS, up from 44 percent; 38 percent of students took Algebra I (important for getting into college), up from 4 percent; 66 percent of students graduated from high school in four years, a city record. And the bad numbers went down. The dropout rate, for example, fell from 9.4 percent in 2007 to 6 percent in 2011. Art and music are back in the schools. Enrollment is higher than it's been in some time. Full-day kindergarten is available for all five-year-olds.

And a program I started my first year as mayor, sending one fifth-grade class every year to see a play downtown, still sparks imaginations. When I was a youngster, I was never exposed to the arts or taken to the theater or museums. When I reached the City Council, I was fortunate enough to be exposed to these things. Boston's kids shouldn't have to wait so long.

"If it can work here, [reform] can work anywhere," Harvard's Jerry Murphy said way back in 1995. The Boston example shows it can. Slowly, without the dramatic gains many parents had hoped for— or, frankly, that I had anticipated from a doubling of the school budget to $775 million and an increase in per-pupil spending to more than $19,000, among the highest of any city school system in the country—slowly, incrementally, unevenly, it worked *here.* The arc of progress is unmistakable in the percentage of tenth-graders passing the MCAS: from 25 percent in 1998 to 86 percent in 2012.

Reform took the kids and the teachers and administrators. It took the voters staying the course. It took Payzant and Johnson and me. It took a city.

• • •

A month before my March 2013 announcement that "I'm not retiring but turning one page of this chapter," Boston closed the book on a bad chapter of its history. A year ahead of the fortieth anniversary of Judge Garrity's court order, the BPS adopted a school assignment plan that strengthens neighborhoods. If that doesn't sound remarkable, you don't know Boston.

On any school day morning, if you stood at the corner of Westville Street and Geneva Avenue in Dorchester, not far from the Burke, you would have seen forty-six different buses picking up 369 different students and transporting them to forty-eight different schools. That was Boston's three-zone school assignment plan at work. Parents had roughly two dozen schools to choose from, with a lottery deciding whether they got their top pick. (My family knew the frustrations of choosing a school: At one point my six grandchildren were all BPS students.) The crazy-quilt transport scheme was a hangover from busing to achieve racial balance. The BPS stopped that kind of busing in the late 90s, when there were too few white kids left in the district to make racial balance feasible.

"Busing" ended. But the buses never stopped rolling, and the dollars kept pouring into gas tanks. In 2009 the district bused five thousand fewer children than it did in 1999 in only five fewer buses. On a quarter of the trips, only a quarter of the buses were full. Of ten buses dropping off students at the Mission Hill School, two carried only one passenger. Nearly empty buses padded a school transportation bill totaling $76 million a year, money subtracted from teaching and learning.

Yet efforts to take the buses off the streets by allowing kids to attend "walk-to" schools were seen by many African American parents as a step backward. To them the "neighborhood school" did not stir memories of the good times before busing but of the racial inequity busing was intended to remedy. They feared the schools in their neighborhoods would never improve. And they resisted changing the child-scattering system of school choice played out every morning at the corner of Westville and Geneva.

That system was destroying neighborhood cohesion. Kids living next door to each other attended different schools. They didn't walk home together. Or share the same teachers or homework. They barely knew each other. In prehistoric Hyde Park, school-based neighborhood friendships were the norm. I wanted Boston's twenty-first-century kids to have what we had then.

As long as most schools were bad and only a few good, the neighborhood school had no chance in Boston. But by 2010, education reform had raised the performance of enough schools to alter the post-busing trade-off of neighborhood schools and solidarity for educational quality and racial equity. My back-to-the-future dream of Hyde Park for all was within reach.

In my 2012 State of the City address I said that "one year from now Boston will have adopted a radically different student assignment plan, one that puts a priority on children attending schools closer to their homes." Guided by the School Committee, I named a twenty-seven-member External Advisory Committee to fulfill my promise. Its task was to come up with a plan that, in a system where not *all* schools were good, would assign kids to a good school close to their homes.

The panel studied the issue for a year, holding over seventy public meetings. While panelists and parents debated the options, Peng Shi could often be seen in the back of the room. An MIT graduate student from Kunming, China, Peng was practicing the Menino method — listening.

Eventually he spoke up: "What I'm hearing is, parents want close to home but they also really care about quality. I'm working on something to try to meet those two goals." He cranked up MIT's computers and they spat out an algorithm. It gave each family a list of six schools to chose from, starting with the two closest high-quality ones, then the next two closest of medium quality. Peng's list combined geography *and* quality. Just what the parents wanted.

The panel had many plans to choose from. In February 2013 it picked Peng Shi's. Unanimously. The vestiges of the school assignment plan that fueled the busing crisis will soon be gone. Busing will no longer break up community in Boston.

> This is the most difficult job I've ever had in my life. . . . The highs and lows come daily. When I haven't been successful at managing the classroom, when I am talking about something I care about, like the civil rights movement, but the students don't share my enthusiasm . . . Ooh, it is a time for pain, a time for crying. . . . There is incredible pain working with students who at times come to school with such great deficits. But the rewards, the affirmations that I belong, come in unexpected ways. After one particularly difficult class, a student wrote me a note that I will save until the day I die. It said: "Miss Powell, we are listening. We are learning. Thank You."
>
> —*Yvonne Powell, teacher at the Jeremiah E. Burke High School. With degrees from Brown, Harvard, and MIT, and a corporate career in finance, planning, and recruiting, the fifty-four-year-old Powell began teaching U.S. and African American history in 2000.*

All good. But what about that symbol of my twenty-year commitment as Boston's "education mayor"? Had the "incremental progress" of the schools reached *that* school?

"There was a real crisis at the Jeremiah Burke," I told the press as early as 1998, when the Burke regained its accreditation. "We had to put extra resources there, and we did. We'll wean them eventually. Now we're putting extra resources into Dorchester High." Which was in danger of losing *its* accreditation. Tom Payzant spoke more bluntly: "The Burke is enriched now beyond other high schools in the city. Not that that's not great, but we can't afford it." Except in unusual cases like the Burke's loss of accreditation, Payzant followed a "formula of equality." All schools would be treated alike. All have the same ratio of staff to students.

Headmaster Steve Leonard hoped that "wouldn't be the last word" on extra help for the Burke. Payzant, he said, didn't "want to believe that this school requires a whole lot more resources than the formula says." To Leonard it was clear that "every time this school gets above . . . a certain number of students, it falls apart."

Two thousand one was the year the Burke sent all its graduating seniors to college. It was also the year that Steve Leonard moved on and funding was cut back to pre-crisis levels. Staff laid off. Enrollment increased.

"Comeback School Holds Its Breath," read a *Globe* headline in November 2002. The story told of rising violence at the Burke. Three teachers had been assaulted. A female student was sent to the hospital after another student "used the heel of her boot as a weapon." Two mothers of feuding students were arrested for fighting with knives in front of the school. "There are a lot of fights," a sophomore boy said. "It's just the way it is."

It was not the way it was a year earlier, when the Burke had nearly two hundred fewer students and twelve more staff to patrol the halls.

In 2006 the Burke was closed for two years for a $49 million reconstruction. A nearby branch library also was due for renovation and expansion. I ordered plans for the separate projects scrapped. Start over, I said. Put library and school together. *Architectural Record* named the reborn Burke, designed by the Boston-based firm Schwartz/Silver Architects, one of its "Schools of the Twenty-first

Century." "The new wing facing Geneva Avenue," it wrote, "gleams like a beacon of possibility in its rugged environment of auto-repair shops and vacant lots." It was the first new facility in my Community Learning Initiative, a citywide program to promote lifelong learning. In 1982 Al Holland, padlocked the doors against the neighborhood. "Today, we reopen the doors to one of the centerpieces of the Grove Hall community," I said at the Burke in 2008, welcoming students and staff to their new building on the first day of school.

That was the good news for the Burke. It had a new school library, cafeteria, kitchen, and gym. It had a performing arts studio, a family center, and renovated science and computer labs. The bad news was that, two years after its award-winning reconstruction, the state's Board of Education found the Burke among "the worst of the worst" schools in Massachusetts. It was threatened with a state takeover. The headmaster was gone and the staff had to reapply for their jobs. Many would not get them back.

I issued a lame statement about the latest crisis in what the *Globe* termed this "barometer of Mayor Thomas M. Menino's effectiveness in improving the city's schools over the past 16 years." What could I say? That I knew how to bring the Burke back but the city couldn't afford it? That it was a question of national priorities? That if the Pentagon would only outspend the next ten countries combined instead of the next fifteen, the Burkes in every American city could work wonders? That we had hit on a formula and proven it twice and just needed the resources to apply it? That's what I should have said.

"There was an earthquake at my school" was how a senior described what happened at the Burke. The wholesale shedding of staff seemed all wrong to him. "When I saw who lost their jobs, it didn't make much sense to me," he told a reporter. "A lot of them were some of the best teachers. . . . What really got to me, though, was that no one, in this whole process, bothered to ask us, the students, what we thought. . . . We know who stays late. We know who calls home, talks to our parents, makes sure we're doing the work. We know who cares about us."

He called Court Street. "I talked to a lady. She was an assistant superintendent or something like that. She said they had a process and everything was done properly, but she said I made a good point about the students being ignored. She said, 'I'll pass on the information and get back to you.' Well it's been two weeks and nobody's called me. I guess they don't care what we think.

"They're looking in the classroom, but they really need to look in the home," he said, surfacing a hard truth about the struggle for the schools. "A lot of the kids who have problems at school have problems at home. But they can't reassign the parents, so they reassign the teachers."

A young woman, also a senior, "was shocked that the Burke was listed as underperforming. I thought, so what does this mean for me? That I am not prepared for college?" Echoing the cheerleader in 1996, at the start of the up-and-down story of the Burke, whose hopes for a scholarship crumbled when the Burke lost its accreditation — echoing the same anxiety about her future as that cheerleader, she asked, "Will the college admission people think twice before accepting me?"

A sign on Tom Payzant's desk read, "What have I done for children today?" The answer is: Not enough. We did not do enough for that young woman. We did not do enough for the young man. It would be small comfort for them to know that we — the people of this rich and powerful country — wanted to do more. We just didn't want it enough.

"I'M NOT A FANCY TALKER"

That was the first sentence I spoke as mayor in January 1994. I was following Tip O'Neill's advice to hang a lantern on your troubles. I couldn't hide my speech troubles if I wanted to.

I'm not unique in American politics. I once read a parody of President Eisenhower delivering the Gettysburg Address that begins, "I haven't checked the figures, but eighty-seven years ago, I think it was, a number of individuals organized a governmental set-up here in this country, I believe it covered eastern areas . . ."

Among mayors, Chicago's Richard J. Daley was a gaffe machine who once praised "Alcoholics Unanimous" and for "tandem bicycle" said "tantrum bicycle." Stan Laurel, of Laurel and Hardy, milked a career of laughs from doing that: "suffering from a nervous shakedown."

"Shakedown" is a "malapropism," for "Mrs. Malaprop," a character in an English comedy who uses the wrong word in place of the right word with a similar sound. I've been called "Mayor Malaprop."

In private conversation I'd usually speak clearly. But put a microphone in front of me and I might say things like "The principal reserves the right to install mental detectors" or "He's the best public service I know" or "We can't just sit in our hands."

"Fred Flintstone. Barney Rubble. And 'Mumbles' Menino makes three," columnist Dave Nyhan once wrote, capturing my voice. In my thick Boston accent "Mayor" was "May-uh," "Commonwealth" "Cawmulth." And I talked out of the side of my mouth. So even when I spoke correctly, I sounded wrong. When I called the lack of parking spaces in Boston "an Alcatraz around my neck," I sounded like Stan Laurel. People didn't feel cruel laughing at me for these howlers because I laughed at myself.

• • •

Over my twenty years in office, Boston's teams won three World Series, three Super Bowls, one NBA championship, and one Stanley Cup. I was frequently called on to salute our local heroes. I did it my way.

Describing a key Red Sox–Yankees playoff battle in 2004, I said, "Davy Roberts stole second base, Mueller hit the double, got him in, then Ortiz won the game. . . . There's so many . . ." I was doing great; then I wandered down memory lane: "Jim Lomborg had the great year he had." Except it was Lonborg, and he pitched for the 1967 Red Sox.

"There's a lot of heart in this team, let me just tell you," I said about the 2012 Celtics. "KJ is great but Hondo is really the inspiration. Hondo drives the team." I meant "KG," for Kevin Garnett, and Rajon Rondo. Memory lane again: "Hondo" was the nickname of Johnny Havlicek, who drove the great Celtics teams of the 60s and 70s.

A press release from City Hall hailing the Bruins for winning the 2011 Stanley Cup would have been ignored. But when I called the Bruins "great ballplayers on the ice and great ballplayers off the ice," it made news.

An embarrassing moment came during a media event for the 2012 Patriots. They were facing a playoff against the Ravens, and I was on the phone betting a lobster on the Pats with the mayor of Baltimore. I said I expected great things from quarterback Tom Brady and nose tackle "Vince Wilcock." Except that his name is Wilfork. Close? Yes, but I was wearing his jersey. With his name on it.

"Menino's Greatest Feat: He Can't Talk About Sports," read a Boston Magazine *headline. Feat? In sports-mad Boston my "often comical ignorance about its sports teams and most popular players" didn't hurt me with voter-fans. I left office with an 83 percent approval rating ("Menino More Popular Than Kittens") because people judged me on the condition of the city, not on the slips of my tongue.*

The truth is, I rarely watched sports — or anything else — on TV. I focused all my attention on the city. Asked about the size of the city budget, Kevin White would make up a number. I knew it to the dollar. Instead of watching sports, maybe Bostonians sensed I was watching out for them. And as my doozies piled up, some observers wondered whether "Menino's . . . comical ignorance" of sports was more comedy than ignorance. The Globe*'s Shirley Leung voiced a growing suspicion: "Menino . . . played us masterfully, knowing a slip of the tongue could generate headlines and sound bites." I kept 'em guessing.*

Chapter 3

Police and Fire

He cared about the community, about the family, and about me. . . . A piece of me died Saturday night. He was a good cop, a good father, a good man, and he was my best friend in the whole world.

— *Officer Robert Luongo, speaking at the funeral of his partner, Berisford Wayne Anderson*

THE TWO WORST things about being mayor? Dead kids and dead cops.

In early February 1994, six weeks after the shooting of honor roll student and anti-gang activist Louis Brown, a few blocks from the church where Louis's funeral was held a policeman was killed. It had been all of two weeks since my swearing-in, yet what I said in my first comment on the tragedy would stay true through every day of my time in office: "The thing that really bothers me about the job is the violence." You don't get used to it. You can't and remain human.

The shooting of Officer Berisford Wayne Anderson contains an infuriating element seen in Boston crimes from the crack craze of the 1980s to the Marathon bombing. His killer was not only known to one branch of law enforcement that failed to communicate with another. It was worse than that. He was actually in jail, awaiting trial for a gun crime, when a prosecutor released him.

The shooting happened around 5:30 on a Saturday afternoon. Anderson had just ended his shift as a plainclothes officer working out of the Area B-3 station, which covers Mattapan and part of Dorchester, where he lived with his fiancée and five children. He went home, took off his bulletproof vest, and left to run a family errand. He had pulled out of his driveway into narrow one-way Spencer Street when he was stopped by a car coming the wrong way.

The driver got out and exchanged words with Anderson, who was stepping from his own car when the driver fired two shots at him. Anderson emptied his .38-caliber revolver firing at his assailant, who, using his car door as a shield, fired back. One of his bullets hit Anderson on the left side. He crumpled on the snow-covered sidewalk a few yards from his front door.

His fiancée ran to him and cradled him in her arms. "He was trying to breathe, trying to talk," she said later. "I told him to hold on, 'don't leave me.'" A neighbor heard her ask, "Who did this?"

Dalton Simpson, eighteen, did it. The whine of his Volkswagen could be heard backing down the length of the street.

Officer Jonathan Stratton was driving nearby when his radio alerted him to watch for a black Volkswagen fleeing the scene of a shooting. Stratton was returning from a cop's funeral. It was for the police chief of a small Massachusetts town. The chief had answered a call for help from police in an adjoining town who were pursuing three burglary suspects. The suspects had fled into the woods. The chief went after them. They shot him as he tried to arrest them.

"I saw the car. I pursued it," Officer Stratton told a reporter. He did not know that the victim was a police officer, much less his former partner.

Stratton's cruiser chased the Volkswagen for about a mile till it sideswiped a parked car on Crowell Street and wound up in a driveway. Simpson got out and ran. Stratton, who had him covered with his gun, ran after him, scrambling over snowbanks and fences. Simpson dropped his gun, a .380-caliber Lorcin (one of 936 guns sold by a Philadelphia gun dealer who didn't keep legally required records). Stratton retrieved it while two other officers tackled Simpson. At a local hospital, where he was treated for injuries sustained during the chase, Simpson, who'd been committing violent crimes for years and getting away with it, said, "I wish I had a bullet for the other cop."

"This is the 90s," Officer Stratton said in an interview. "Things have changed. There's no respect for police anymore, especially with young kids. Their whole culture is to hate cops. It's in their music and their videos." "Cop Killer" and "Fuck the Police" were high on the hit parade. The music industry was making millions off targeting policemen.

Three months before his fatal run-in with Anderson, Simpson was arrested in Framingham, twenty miles west of Boston, for trading shots with a drug dealer. He was jailed for a month. Then an assistant district attorney got a bright idea: to waive his $10,000 bail if Simpson testified against the dealer. Simpson agreed, but failed to keep his end of the bargain — to appear in Framingham District Court in early December.

There is a haunting might-have-been to Officer Anderson's murder. Anderson volunteered to help kids in his neighborhood stay straight. Among other good works, he led a troop of Police Explorers, an offshoot of the Boy Scouts. Nearly all of his life Simpson lived one street over from Anderson. Simpson was born in Jamaica. Anderson was the son of a Jamaican immigrant. That was a bridge between the kid and the cop. Could Anderson have crossed it if he had found Simpson in time? No kid is destined to be a killer.

What to do about kids who kill? I called for "early childhood education programs that work on a kid's self-esteem — to get down to the basics of how we deal with the problem," and for more investment in neighborhood programs and summer jobs. Does that sound like a "bleeding-heart liberal"? Then listen to the cops. When he first met with the BPD's anti-gang unit, my new police commissioner expected to hear "more cops," "tougher judges," "more jails." But what they said was "We need more jobs and alternatives for these kids."

Jobs and alternatives for kids: Through two decades that was key to my strategy on crime prevention. Our summer jobs program steered teenagers away from the streets. But we needed to reach their younger brothers and sisters, too, to keep them from gangs, drugs, and violence. I jump ahead here to fill in that piece of the story.

I had a crazy idea. Suburban kids go to summer camp. Why not city kids?

Suburban families pay the $3,000-per-month cost of camp. City families need help. It is justified. Preventing crime is a public good. Nothing was stopping me from sending Boston's kids to camp. Nothing except for the money to rent the camp, transport and feed the kids, and pay the salaries of instructors, lifeguards, nurses, and kitchen workers.

In 2007 I was uncertain whether to run for a fifth term in 2009, and if I ran, whether I'd win. Before it was too late, I had to see my crazy idea into the world.

Camp Harbor View partly owes its existence to something a Roxbury youngster told me: He had just learned in school that Boston bordered on the ocean. He had never seen "the water" himself.

That got me thinking about some land the city owned on the water — Long Island, a narrow peninsula sticking into Boston Harbor. Up until the 50s, the city ran a hospital there for patients suffering from chronic illnesses. In recent times the hospital was used as a homeless shelter and drug treatment facility. Beyond the building stretched twelve acres of bare land surrounded by water. It was just about the choicest site in Boston, with views across the harbor to the downtown skyline.

But the harbor — if you fell into it, you'd come out with a disease. By 1988 it was so polluted that the GOP presidential candidate, George H. W. Bush, exploited it as an issue against his Democratic opponent, Massachusetts governor Michael Dukakis. Through the 90s, the Commonwealth spent billions cleaning the harbor. By 2007 it was safe to put a summer camp on Long Island.

Somebody should write a book about what cities owe to rich people. The Boston chapter would feature benefactors going back to the eighteenth century. My friend Jack Connors belongs in that company. Jack grew up in Boston. He made a fortune in advertising in Boston. When he retired, he decided to give back.

Jack's Rolodex is a who's who of the generous rich. I showed him the Long Island land and asked him to raise the money to put a summer camp there. I had him with the anecdote about the kid who'd never seen the ocean.

The media was forever poking into my so-called pet contractors, looking for dirt. There was no dirt. But there was loyalty from companies like Suffolk Construction that had done all right building in Boston. I told Suffolk I needed a camp in a hurry; and with workers sleeping in tents on the site, in 109 days it was done. On July 2, 2007, Camp Harbor View welcomed its first three hundred campers.

Run by the Boys & Girls Clubs of Boston, the camp teaches kids eleven to fourteen swimming (in an Olympic-sized pool), sailing, and kayaking. Arts, crafts, softball, soccer, and fitness round out the picture. Older kids training to be counselors take classes in math and English. A staff of seventy-five counselors, a social worker, and a nurse look after about eight hundred kids—half in July, half in August. School buses pick the kids up before eight A.M. and drop them off at home at six, with a boxed supper so their mothers don't have to rush home from work to cook.

The official cost is $5 a month. But I didn't want kids who paid ragging those who couldn't, so nobody collects it. Even kids have dignity.

"Crossing the bridge onto this island and looking at the city from afar is symbolic," a counselor who'd started as a camper told a reporter. "You realize there's so much more to learn and experience beyond the confines of your neighborhood." I hope that kid who didn't know about the ocean got a chance to take in that view, to see those wider horizons.

The dining hall is named after one Mayor Thomas M. Menino. Fifty years from now kids won't know who that was. Maybe someone will explain, "He was a guy from Hyde Park who wanted you to have fun, learn stuff, and return from camp at the end of the day too tired to get into trouble."

Politicians can't resist demagoguing crime. Governor Bill Weld, for example. His response to Wayne Anderson's killing was to call for Massachusetts to restore the death penalty. His Democratic opponent in that year's governor's race also came out for death. In Wash-

At Doyle's in Jamaica Plain with Mayor Ray Flynn and former mayor Kevin White when I was a city councilor.
Courtesy of the Menino Family

On a panel with President Bill Clinton to discuss the Community Oriented Policing Services (COPS) grant in 1994. Community policing reminded me of the neighborhood cops on the beat in Hyde Park in the 1950s. *Joanne Rathe*/The Boston Globe/*Getty Images*

After the panel, at lunch with President Clinton and Senator Ted Kennedy at Mike's City Diner, which was a cash-only place. I picked up the tab.

John Tlumacki/The Boston Globe/*Getty Images*

From the *Boston Globe Magazine*'s December 4, 1994, cover story: "Boston's Urban Mechanic: Can Mayor Menino's Nuts-and-Bolts Approach Revive the City?"

Bill Greene /The Boston Globe

I gave out honors to students for academic achievement and for school spirit—putting the spotlight on kids who had never won anything before—for twenty-nine years.

Courtesy of the City of Boston

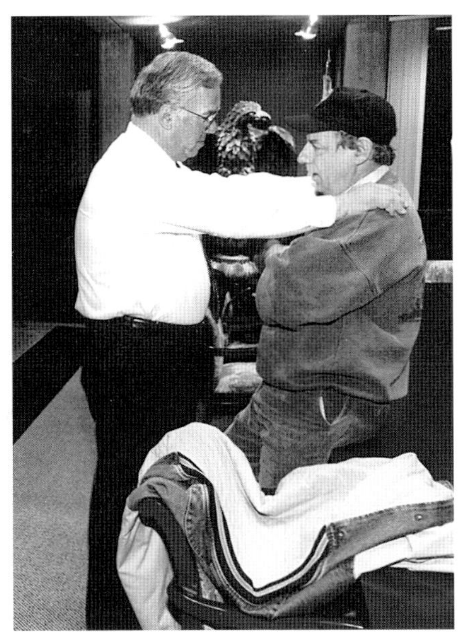

Vote No on Question 2. With my friend Bob "Skinner" Donahue on the night we won the referendum for an appointed school committee, November 1996.
*Michael Robinson-Chavez/*The Boston Globe*/ Getty Images*

At the Curtis Guild School in East Boston with Bill Cosby, the co-chair of the Massachusetts Service Summit for Net Day 3, on October 25, 1997. The Boston public schools were the first in the country to be wired for the Internet. *© Don West Photography*

My granddaughter Giulia Fenton playing under my desk at City Hall. When I first took office I didn't have any grandchildren. When I left I had six. *Courtesy of the City of Boston*

The Geneva Avenue walk in Dorchester was a Christmas tradition.
Courtesy of the City of Boston

With Karen Marinella of WLVI-TV at the Democratic National Convention in 2004. Bringing the convention to Boston, a Democratic city in a blue state, was a big deal.
Courtesy of the City of Boston

Marching in the Gay Pride parade. On my left is Harry Collings, a longtime friend and an advisor on LGBT issues. *Courtesy of the City of Boston*

Visiting Camp Harbor View, a haven for inner-city kids. *Courtesy of the City of Boston*

The 2008 Christmas toy drive for the Bowdoin-Geneva neighborhood. By my last year in office we were delivering toys to four thousand families. *Courtesy of the City of Boston*

Speaking at Faneuil Hall shortly after taking the oath of office for a historic fifth term, surpassing Kevin White's record. *Courtesy of the City of Boston*

The support and love of my family, and knowing I would have more time for my grandkids, made my decision not to run again, after serving for twenty years, a little easier.
Barry Chin / The Boston Globe / *Getty Images*

The part of being mayor that I miss the most is being with the city's kids. *Courtesy of the City of Boston*

Boston Strong. Six months after the Marathon bombing, Red Sox slugger David Oritz's son D'Angelo celebrates the World Series win at Fenway Park.
Courtesy of the City of Boston

With my wife, Angela, at the Hyde Park YMCA, which was named in my honor. I came here often as a kid and still live nearby. *Suzanne Kreiter/*The Boston Globe*/Getty Images*

A private moment in the Oval Office with President Obama and Vice Pesident Biden.

Courtesy of the White House Photo Office

ington the Democratic Senate was debating President Bill Clinton's tough crime bill. It included welcome money to hire more cops in Boston, but set aside only $100 million for neighborhood programs.

That represented less than 1 percent of the bill's $23 billion cost. Suppose 25 percent of the $23 billion had gone into early childhood education and basketball leagues and mentors and summer jobs instead of prisons and high-tech equipment for the police. I think crime would have fallen sharply. But until you prove them wrong, politicians will cling to the cynical wisdom that there are no votes in preventing crime, only in punishing it.*

With or without federal aid, Boston would lead the country in preventing crime. And we would do it without searching "suspicious" young African American men—the controversial policy known as "stop and frisk." I would not tolerate racial profiling. You can't police a multiracial city like an occupying army.

Just before he left on his Roman holiday, Ray Flynn appointed a new police commissioner. Hired in the summer of 1993, Bill Bratton was gone by winter, lured to New York by Rudy Giuliani. Naming Bratton's replacement was my call, the most important appointment of

* From my interview with Katie Couric on the *Today* show, May 17, 1994:

KATIE COURIC: You know, you're a lone voice in another area, welfare reform. That's a big cause right now across the country and in . . . Massachusetts. Governor Weld has cut the number of people on the rolls dramatically. He wants to cut an additional seventy thousand families. And you're a public official who is saying, "Whoa! Wait a minute . . ."

MAYOR MENINO: It's another one of those things [like crime]. While there are welfare cheats—do all those young women and men want to be on welfare? Probably not. . . . If we cut welfare, where do they go? They go to the streets, and they go into the shelters. . . . Let's have a comprehensive plan . . . to get people off welfare and [into] jobs—job training programs, attracting new industries to this state and this country. . . . We can't just say we're going to cut welfare for the sake of headlines. Let's get real about it. The problem is that we—we tend, as elected officials, to worry more about headlines than really doing something for people.

my mayoralty. Officer Anderson's death delayed my decision for a week.

The search committee forwarded the names of four finalists. Two would have made history. Boston police superintendent Joseph C. Carter would have been Boston's first African American police commissioner. Massachusetts State Police lieutenant colonel Kathleen O'Toole would have been — and eventually was — the first woman to hold the job. The other candidates were former Chicago police commander Dennis Nowicki and Boston's acting police commissioner, Paul Evans, Bratton's former deputy.

During the '93 campaign any member of my team who referred to me publicly as "acting mayor" didn't do it a second time. I wanted voters to forget about the "acting" part. Still, why kid myself? I wouldn't have been elected mayor without my five-month tryout.

As a chief executive, I liked acting positions. People want to prove they can do the job. They're not "acting"— they're working hard to win a permanent appointment.

Paul Evans had been acting police commissioner for barely a month when Officer Anderson's death threw us together.

We sat together in the front pew of the Charles Street AME Church for Anderson's funeral. Together we joined in the applause for Anderson's eight commendations for bravery. Together we nodded as we heard Reverend Mickari D. Thomas Jr., a Boston police chaplain, declare, "In a time when we desperately need role models for our young people, Officer Anderson was just that." We were moved when Anderson's partner, Officer Robert Luongo, after reading his handwritten remarks, plunged off the pulpit, gently patted Anderson's coffin, and hurried back to his pew, where he broke into sobs that echoed through the church. In the snow of Forest Hills Cemetery we struggled to control our emotions as Officer Michael Fish played "Taps." Together we went to the grave to comfort Anderson's mother, Edainey Matthews Blissett, sobbing in her son Ronald's arms, and the rest of the family. An immigrant family of the New America who gave their son to protect the city.

Paul Evans was born and raised in a blue-collar family in South Boston, where he went to school, played sports, met his wife, Karen (at a "sock hop"), and always lived. In 1968 he and five buddies from his corner enlisted in the Marine Corps; all served in Vietnam; only four came back. Paul joined the Boston Police in 1970. He soon found himself pitted against many of his neighbors, enforcing Judge Garrity's order to integrate South Boston High School. While rising through the ranks, he earned a law degree.

Paul and I were basically the same type of public person, low-key, and just wanted to get the job done. Calling for "collaboration," "partnerships," and "taking responsibility," he sang from my hymnal. No Bratton, he was somewhat shy, another trait we shared.

Even if I'd known none of this, I might have offered Paul Evans the job anyway, from observing him in the days after the murder of one of his men. He was at all times, but especially at the funeral, calm, caring, tactful, and dignified. You're impressed when someone displays qualities you try to display yourself.

"Although Menino appears to have made up his mind days ago, he reportedly has confided in no one, not even his wife," Chris Black wrote in the *Boston Sunday Globe*, three days after the Anderson funeral. I know how seriously I took the decision. But did I keep it from Angela, and how would Chris know? That evening I called Evans and ordered him to be at my house in Readville in a half hour. He made it in less time. When I said he could drop the "acting," he beamed.

"I think we will be a good team," I told reporters. We were.

Under Paul Evans the BPD implemented a new crime prevention strategy that had the law enforcement community and the White

House hailing the "Boston miracle" as a national model. That helped to restore the sunken reputation of the nation's oldest police department. Evans, I promised the city, would initiate "a lot of changes in the way policemen do their work." Critics worried that his longevity in the department made him an unlikely candidate to change it, but I saw it the other way: As a committed BPD lifer, he'd have greater credibility to press for reform than an outsider. "Paul Evans will not be status quo," I said.

In the Boston Police Department the status quo was unacceptable.

> Police recruits get the first taste of the inefficient institution they are about to enter when they take a six week course at the Police Academy, an abandoned school in Hyde Park outfitted with furniture fit for fifth graders. . . . The most modern piece of equipment is a machine intended to simulate situations in which an officer may fire his handgun. But the commission discovered that the gun used is a revolver that the department abandoned a few years ago in favor of a newer model. Like much else in the department, the intention is good, the execution faulty.
>
> —*from a 1992* Boston Globe *editorial, "A Blueprint to Improve the Police," on the findings of the St. Clair Commission*

When Paul took over, the department was in crisis, beset by mismanagement at the top and misconduct in the ranks.

Its highest officers owed their jobs to cronyism. Ray Flynn had named his best friend police commissioner: Francis "Mickey" Roache was a sergeant when Flynn elevated him. Five members of Roache's command staff held the civil service rank of "patrolman." Three deputy superintendents were former Flynn drivers. The perception that the mayor ran the department undermined Roache's authority among the rank and file. And as even Flynn conceded, Roache was a poor administrator.

"A lot of people are taking shots at Mickey Roache, but I don't think Ray Flynn sees him as a burden," I said as a city councilor in 1991. "Loyalty matters too much to the mayor."

Flynn stood by his friend even as judges, prosecutors, and the media assailed the department's handling of two notorious murder cases.

The first was the shooting of Detective Sherman Griffiths in a 1988 drug raid. A member of the department's elite Drug Control Unit, Griffiths was swinging a sledgehammer against the door of a Dorchester apartment when the drug dealer inside fired through it. Superior Court judge Charles M. Grabau dismissed the murder charge against the alleged shooter because the evidence was "tainted" by "egregious" police misconduct. The detectives had no "probable cause" for conducting the search. They acted under a warrant based on the testimony of an informant they had invented. "John" had helped them obtain over fifty other warrants.

Because of the illegality of the raid and blunders in the murder investigation, Officer Sherman Griffiths's killer was never prosecuted.

The use of dubious informants was widespread. The *Globe* revealed that forty of forty-four search warrants issued to another detective cited the same informant. This guy got around. He infiltrated drug operations in Allston, Brighton, Dorchester, Jamaica Plain, Mattapan, and Roxbury, "variously befriending dealers who were white, black, Hispanic, and, in one case, Cuban." Altogether, the Drug Control Unit relied on only twelve informants for more than two hundred warrants.

"It's like someone in your business making up a quote," a cop explained to a reporter. "Everybody knows it's done all the time."

The second case became a national sensation. A white couple, Carol and Charles Stuart, had just left a birthing class at a Boston hospital. They were driving through Roxbury, en route to their suburban home, when a black man forced his way into their car at a stoplight, ordered them to go to a Mission Hill housing development, and, after robbing them, shot Carol dead and wounded Charles. That was the story Charles Stuart gave police.

Bowing to protests from the African American community, the police had recently curtailed their stop-and-frisk policy. With charges of police brutality still in the air, Deputy Superintendent Paul Evans urged caution in the search for the shooter.

But frenzied media coverage of the murder of a mother and unborn child pressured City Hall to order every available detective to find the killer. One hundred officers swarmed over the Mission Main development, stopping and frisking and grilling young black men.

After Stuart identified Willie Bennett, a Mission Main resident with a criminal record, as the perpetrator, several detectives ran amok. They planted what appeared to be drugs on would-be witnesses to coerce them to testify against Bennett and threatened other witnesses with beatings and prison sentences. Predictably, they furnished false information to obtain two search warrants.

On this manufactured evidence, the Suffolk County district attorney was set to indict Bennett for first-degree murder when Charles Stuart jumped off the Tobin Bridge and the world learned that he was the murderer.

After a fifteen-month investigation into possible civil rights violations by the police, U.S. Attorney Wayne A. Budd found "strong evidence of serious misconduct," but was unable to prove that the police were "intentionally trying to deprive Bennett and the witnesses of their civil rights by building a case against Bennett while knowing he was not the killer."

Budd, an African American appointed by President George H. W. Bush, spoke for the city when he said, "The whole case has been tragic, including the fact that a community of color was falsely blamed for this crime."

Budd's inquiry ran into a "blue wall" of silence around the Bennett investigation. Shielding wrongdoing was a chronic problem in the BPD. The blue wall shielded cops who got rough making arrests. In several news-making instances it protected cops who killed fleeing or, so eyewitnesses claimed, unarmed suspects.

The citizen's only recourse against police brutality was to appeal to the Internal Affairs Division. But the blue wall extended to Internal Affairs, which found for the accused policeman 98 percent of the time.

Responding to a drumbeat of revelations, Mayor Flynn convened a blue-ribbon commission to "review the basic management and supervision systems and practices of the Boston Police Department." The chairman was James D. St. Clair, a senior figure of the Boston Bar and President Richard M. Nixon's lawyer during Watergate.

The headline recommendation of St. Clair's 150-page report was that Commissioner Roache must go: "Despite nearly seven years at the helm, Commissioner Roache has failed to develop and articulate a shared vision or strategic plan to guide the department's operations."

The police would not police themselves: "Officers with a long record of alleged misconduct, including some with histories of alleged physical abuse of citizens, remain on the street largely unidentified and unsupervised."

To lessen the distrust between police and public, the commission proposed a new strategy of policing. A strategy that "would thrust Boston into the forefront of American police departments." I charged the search committee for the new police commissioner to send me candidates committed to this strategy.

"Neighborhood policing" stirred my memories of "the Deacon." I had a vision of cops on the beat stopping to help grandmothers up stairs, of cops taking bullies aside and asking how they'd feel if the bigger kids pushed *them* around, of cops exchanging summer evening greetings with folks sitting on their front porches.

Paul Evans remembered two Deacons, Gene Dumas and John Kelly, from his South Boston youth: "Those cops knew everybody and everybody knew them. . . . Everybody talked to them, and everybody trusted them." When neighbors complained about Evans and his friends playing football on the street, "Dumas and Kelly would take the football, and if their order to play in the park were obeyed, the football would be returned." Order. Obeyed. Those were the days.

Was my vision an attack of nostalgia for the Hyde Park of the 50s? Or was community policing another back-to-the-future moment, a chance for Boston's twenty-first-century kids to grow up with a measure of the security that Paul and I took for granted as kids? As a former officer of the National Trust for Historic Preservation, I believe in preserving the past for the future. I believe that about the public goods of the city as well as its public face. About society as well as architecture. Progress is not abandoning the past but recovering its richness and spreading the wealth to new circumstances and new people.

Repudiating his own commission ("I know more about the neighborhoods than Mr. St. Clair"), Flynn appointed Roache to another five-year term but, acknowledging his management shortcomings, named Bill Bratton, then head of security for the transit authority (the "T"), "superintendent in chief."

The St. Clair Commission issued thirty-six separate recommendations in areas ranging from internal affairs to information technology. Bratton moved to implement thirty-one of them, including neighborhood policing, beginning a pilot program in Dorchester.

The two-headed BPD divided into two camps: one for Roache and the status quo; one for Bratton and change. Paul Evans sided with the reformers. Roache stopped speaking to him. Bratton got more drastic treatment: Commissioner Roache barricaded the door connecting his office with the superintendent in chief's.

After Roache resigned to run for mayor, Boston had Bratton's attention for only a few weeks when New York came calling. Paul Evans inherited a divided and drifting department. My mandate to him was to close the breach that the Stuart case had opened between the police and the African American community.

> The "new day" [will be] the one where Menino's police forces do not confuse a vomiting senior citizen with Jaws.
>
> —Globe *columnist Derrick Z. Jackson commenting on a tragic police shooting*

The Reverend Accelynne Williams had made pancakes for breakfast and some of the mix spilled on the kitchen table of his Dorchester apartment. The seventy-five-year-old retired Methodist minister from Antigua, a leader of the resistance against drugs in the Caribbean, was sitting at the table when his front door flew off its hinges and thirteen battering-ram-bearing, shotgun-wielding, shield-carrying members of a SWAT team burst in. A cop screamed, "White substance on the table. Get him!" and the black-helmeted wave rolled forward. Williams fled to his bedroom and locked the door. His age and frailty did not suggest to the SWAT team that perhaps they had invaded the wrong apartment. Shattering the bedroom door with the battering ram, they rushed in. They found Reverend Williams "in a crouch position" in the corner, handcuffed him, and threw him to the floor. He began to vomit and soon died of a heart attack.

"I hope you've had a great day," Paul Evans said when he called me with the news. "Because it's about to turn terrible."

At a press conference that afternoon, Paul characterized what happened in the apartment as "a struggle." Then he had the decency to add, "I'm not going to say it was an intense struggle."

Neighborhood policing was off to a bad start.

Sherman Griffiths's shooting cast a shadow over Reverend Williams's death. Before Griffiths, the procedure was to shout "Police, open the door!" But Griffiths's warning shout cost him his life. So the procedure was changed. No warning, and instead of detectives, a SWAT team to take the door. Charles Stuart's damnable lie and the heavy-handed dragnet for the black killer cast a deeper shadow. "This leads everyone back to Stuart," said Bruce Wall, a Dorchester minister, meaning the SWAT team's scaring Williams to death. "It's still raw."

That's why, addressing an NAACP banquet that night, I apologized for this senseless tragedy, and why I urged Paul Evans, less than twenty-four hours after his first defensive statement, to strike a healing note.

First he called Reverend Williams's widow, Mary, for a painful conversation. Some of his advisers thought he should make no public statement until after the incident was investigated. Any admission of responsibility might expose the city to a lawsuit. (It did: We reached an agreement with Mary Williams for $1 million, the biggest settlement in Boston history.) Then he appeared before the cameras and, for the 1,900 men and women of the Boston Police Department, he apologized to the black community.

A confidential informant with a good track record, Evans said, was certain "there were drugs and guns at that location." Reverend Williams's apartment was on the second floor. The warrant specified the third floor. The floor plan confused the SWAT team. "There was a tragic mistake."

After watching Evans on television, a black political consultant remarked, "I said, 'This is different.' For the Police Commissioner to say, 'I'm sorry,' is an extraordinary thing." Because Evans quickly recovered from his stumble, said the Reverend Charles Stith, a prominent South End pastor, "people are willing to give him the benefit of the doubt."

"This is the first time I've seen a mayor and a police commissioner come out and apologize," said Reverend Wall.

The SWAT team's invasion of the wrong apartment showed the need for better advance information about where the bad guys really were. Neighborhood policing was not social work but law enforcement. It was about residents helping the police protect them. Transparency was the first step. The police couldn't hide their blunders and expect to be trusted with tips about neighborhood criminals. Paul's apology demonstrated that change had come to the Boston Police Department.

Neighborhood policing was now off to a good start.

> For the last twenty years, we've been too busy answering 911 calls, helter-skelter, all over the place . . . to get to know peo-

> ple. We got in cruisers and stopped walking around. . . . It tore down the whole sense of accountability and responsibility. Technology actually hurt us. It gave us the 911 system, in which everybody just went to the next call. And while we were breaking down, so were the institutions that had stabilized us.
>
> —*Boston Police Commissioner Paul Evans, speaking to a community meeting in Codman Square*

After the Bell Telephone Company introduced the 911 universal emergency call system in the late 60s, police departments competed over "rapid response," defined as "the time between dispatch of the call and the officers' arrival on the scene." The BPD came up with its own in-house metric, "zero cars available" (meaning no patrol cars were free), which measured how long *all* cars in a police district were tied up answering calls. "Since Zero Car Availability was considered a negative, this measure created an artificial pressure to 'clear the call as quickly as possible' to be available for the next one," a report concluded. "Many officers attempted to meet this departmental directive, but it came at the cost of minimizing effective interaction with the citizens."

"Next call, next cruiser" made police strangers in the neighborhoods. It was past time for a new way of policing.

The first step: months of planning and neighborhood-by-neighborhood organization under Strategic Planning teams led by the captains of Boston's eleven police districts. The captains recruited team members from the neighborhoods—activists, church leaders, business owners, youth service workers. The members asked their neighbors to identify the most serious neighborhood problems, and together set "realistic goals" for solving them.

The planning teams agreed on goals reflecting local realities. For example:

- Create safe business districts in South Boston.
- Reduce larceny from motor vehicles in West Roxbury.
- Make the drug culture less attractive via positive community values.

Goals were then narrowed to specific objectives:

- Reduce the number of complaints about public drinking.
- Increase drug arrests in the district by 10 percent.
- Increase parental responsibility and parents' awareness of the actions of their children.

The U.S. Justice Department called Boston's blueprint for neighborhood policing "as comprehensive as any you will find."

In the districts, meanwhile, officers were assigned to patrol set areas. The same twelve to fifteen officers spread over three shifts patrolling the same ten- to twelve-block area. Day after day. Week after week. Mostly in cars; sometimes on foot. Long enough to become known and trusted.

Their job was not to respond to crimes but to prevent them by fixing the neighborhood's "broken windows"—vandalism, abandoned cars, public drinking, graffiti. Crime could fall statistically, but if people didn't feel safe, the numbers didn't matter. And if people didn't feel safe, they went out less, and the streets became more dangerous. Removing the eyesores of disorder signaled that the streets did not belong to lawbreakers.

Surveys confirmed that neighborhood policing had made a difference. A man I ran into on Dorchester's Geneva Avenue could hardly believe it: "Mayor, its amazing—no more gunshots." As I put it in my 1997 State of the City address, "Today, everyone can feel safer on our streets—except the criminals."

"Ten years ago the city paid lip service to community policing," a civilian on one of the Strategic Planning teams told researchers. "Cops were only visiting the businesses they knew. We had one officer who would park illegally in a bus stop and then sit all day in a single coffee shop. This shop got excellent police protection, but the rest of the business district suffered. Now we have a bicycle officer who is very mobile. He isn't in a car, he is moving, he is friendly. It is no longer us versus them."

Another team member said: "The Strategic Planning effort was an exercise in process and patience, but it was well worth it. The change between the community and police is evident. They came out of the cars, moved to walking beats — it has been a 180 degree change. Dorchester is a vast area and there are many neighborhood associations and meetings. Our concerns are not falling on deaf ears."

Responsibility for public safety was shifted from headquarters to the station house, from the station house to the squad car, from the squad car to the walking cop, from the cop to the citizen.

> Officers and residents across the nation have offered testimonials about how successful community policing partnerships have improved their lives; one police officer summed it up by noting that kids now waved to him using all five fingers instead of just one.
>
> *—from the "Boston Police Department's Strategic Planning Process: Phase One, Final Report"*

"Now we're going into the neighborhoods, meeting with residents and making them feel like they have a part in the crime issue," I told *USA Today* in 1996. We asked people to take responsibility for their neighborhoods — for each other — and they stepped up.

To draw attention to a spike in nighttime disorder in the Back Bay, neighbors held a camp-out in a park. Jamaica Plain residents requested that one team meeting a month be conducted in Spanish to allow their Spanish-speaking neighbors to attend. Because meetings were held after work, some folks didn't have time for supper. So those who could brought potluck dishes to meetings and fed their neighbors.

There was pushback from civilians. Under 911 policing, you reported something stolen from your house, within a few hours a cop would be at your door. Under the new strategy, if the officer assigned to your neighborhood was on vacation, you might wait several days.

There was pushback from the police. "This isn't why I became a cop. If I wanted to become a social worker, I wouldn't have gone through the academy." That view was out there.

The department figured that young cops would adapt to the new strategy easier than old-timers, but some veteran cops liked its back-to-the-future flavor. "I've been on the job for 32 years now," said one. "I came on the job when cops did what we're trying to get back to doing. I believe in this neighborhood policing. . . . It gives people a sense of safety, of control. They can approach us, we're a sounding board. If you take care of the little things the bigger things take care of themselves."

That veteran was among the first cops to practice neighborhood policing. He and his partner worked a pilot program in Roxbury's Academy Homes. They befriended nine-year-old Jermaine Goffigan. He invited the two officers to his ninth birthday party on Halloween. They stopped by and wished him well.

Twenty minutes after they left the party, Jermaine was dead, gunned down in a gang crossfire as he stood in front of his home.

Jermaine Goffigan. I named a park after him.* He was out trick-or-treating in a Dracula mask. Police found five Tootsie Rolls and a lemon drop in his pockets. Who could have guessed that Boston was about to go two and a half years without losing another Jermaine? Not a single kid killed in twenty-nine months.

That was the "Boston miracle" celebrated by the national media and saluted by President Clinton.

That, and this: In 1995 there were ninety-six homicides in Boston, fifty-nine in 1996, forty-three in 1997, and thirty-five in 1998.

And this: In 1995 Boston's crime rate ranked it twenty-eighth lowest among the fifty largest cities, twenty-second in 1996, and twelfth in 1997.

So crime was down. One of the objectives laid out in the 1995 Boston Neighborhood Policing Initiative was met.

A second objective was to reduce fear of crime. In a 1997 BPD survey, 75 percent of Boston residents said they felt "very safe" at home at night. Nationally, only 43 percent of city dwellers felt "very safe."

The third objective was to improve the quality of life in the neighborhoods. Here the results were less impressive but still encouraging. The proportion of Bostonians calling graffiti a serious neighborhood problem was "significantly lower than the national sample," and "a smaller portion of Bostonians than Chicagoans believe that graffiti, drug dealing, public drinking, and abandoned cars are a serious problem in their neighborhood."

Crime fell everywhere in the 90s, but faster and lower in practically every category in Boston. A puzzling exception: Triple the

* In June 2002 Trina Persad was playing in Jermaine Goffigan Park when a stray bullet hit her. "We as a government can put program after program in place," I told the press. "But there has to be some sense of caring and a focus from parents on their children." I visited Trina at the Boston Medical Center. She hung on for two days. She was ten years old.

percentage of Bostonians than city residents nationwide said "dogs running loose" was a serious neighborhood problem.

The St. Clair Commission advocated neighborhood policing to restore public confidence in a Roache-era BPD that ranked twenty-eighth out of thirty major cities in solving murders and twenty-seventh in arrests for felonies like rape and robbery. Two years into the new strategy, 84 percent of Boston residents had a "great deal" or "some" confidence that the police could prevent crime, compared to 58 percent of the national sample.

Perhaps surprisingly, the police had embraced neighborhood policing. Whereas only 17 percent listed arresting criminals or reducing crime as their prime goal, 68 percent listed goals like "helping people/making them feel safe."

Except for those wild dogs, all the trends were good.

"We're working together for the first time," I said, referring generally to police-community cooperation and specifically to a partnership between Boston police and state agencies.

Between 1990 and 1995, a quarter of offenders in murder cases were on parole at the time of their offense. Parolees bore watching, but no one was watching them. Under Operation Nightlight, Boston police officers teamed with Massachusetts probation officers to make nightly visits to the homes of high-risk offenders to see if they were observing the terms of their parole — 2,500 visits in 1996. These bed checks gave parents and grandparents welcome leverage to keep their young men off the streets. Cooperation from families helped make Nightlight work. According to the FBI *Law Enforcement Bulletin,* "Going from zero supervisory visits to thousands each year made a substantial impact on the comparatively small number of offenders causing the most problems."

Representatives from eighty cities visited Boston to see how we did it. "We're stealing every idea that Boston hasn't locked down," said a Minneapolis police lieutenant after his visit. "Look what happened to your body count. . . . You're doing something right."

Then the police union and Democratic politicians set progress back.

I believe in unions. They put the American Dream within reach of men like my dad, a member of the Machinists Union.

So it pained me when the Boston police union impeded neighborhood policing.*

I also believe in the values of the Democratic Party. However, I was ashamed of my party for a vote cast by the overwhelmingly Democratic Massachusetts state legislature.

The vote repealed a century-old law allowing Boston's police commissioner to make personnel decisions affecting public safety without negotiating with the police unions. Paul Evans needed that flexibility to implement the new strategy. In practice that could mean assigning younger officers to jobs veterans (wrongly) considered "RIP" (retired in place) and wanted as a benefit of their seniority. The Boston Police Patrolmen's Association (BPPA) could not tolerate that. So its political action committee (PAC) donated heavily to the lawmakers' campaigns, and the Democrats voted to forbid Evans from changing deployments without union approval.

Citing Boston's record in reducing crime, Governor Paul Cellucci, a Republican, vetoed the Democratic bill. "I do not believe that it is in the best interest of the Commonwealth," he said, "and, in particular, the citizens of Boston, to change the existing relationship between management and labor when the public safety could suffer."

* I was a pro-union mayor. For example, I took the side of SEIU janitors in their struggle for higher wages and better health care, helping settle a 2002 strike on terms favorable to the janitors.

I lobbied state senators to sustain Cellucci's veto. I argued these points:

1. Neighborhood policing worked.
2. Management flexibility made it work.
3. A vote against management flexibility was therefore a vote against the "Boston miracle."

I was wasting my breath. Every Democrat voted to override the governor's veto.

One of my aides drew the moral: "Get me a PAC and a checkbook and I'll get some votes too. What are we going to do, not give out any passes for the Marathon this year?"

The override came in January 1998. That year, the miracle faded. Kids started killing other kids again. Boston's crime rate ticked up. Was the legislature's meddling in neighborhood policing *the* cause? No. Was it *a* cause? Undoubtedly.

"Relations between City Hall and the police, frayed by contract negotiations and the police commissioner bill, have reached an all-time low," the *Globe* observed. Shortly after the vote, free copies of *Pax Centurion,* the newspaper of the Boston Police Patrolmen's Association, were missing from their usual places in City Hall and had to be restocked.

I had a tough relationship with the BPPA. Every time the police contract was up for renewal, pickets dogged me. One year, a dozen officers showed up in front of the National Press Club in Washington, where I was speaking. "I'm laying off 1,700 people, and they're asking for a raise," I told the audience. "I just don't have it." And BPPA picket lines nearly stopped the 2004 Democratic National Convention, which, for the first time, was held in Boston.

Ahead of the 2004 negotiations, the union played hardball. BPPA

President Tom Nee promised that six-member squads of off-duty officers would follow me to all events. For parades, the contingent would be tripled. I increased my personal security just in case. A hell of a note: on-duty police protecting the mayor from their off-duty brothers.

But it gets worse. Any BPPA member who refused to picket me, Nee announced, would lose dental coverage, life insurance, the right to legal services, and other benefits. Who was this threat aimed at? Nee said at slackers. I had my doubts. What cop, I wondered, wouldn't picket me? I could think of only one — Officer Thomas M. Menino Jr. Was the union pressuring him to picket his father?

Picketing policemen cursed me. Picketing firemen spat on Angela. Fire was that much worse than police.

We die for you.

— Captain John J. McKenna of the Boston Fire Department in an August 2002 letter to the editor of the Boston Globe

Captain McKenna continued: "Now men and women who are willing to die for you are often unable to articulate the reasons why they undertake these risks for you except for their strong sense of duty. . . . Our strong points aren't community relations."

Give me a break! Try negotiating with a union whose members die for you. Above the windows of Memorial Hall at BFD headquarters were two rows of photographs of firefighters killed in the line of duty. They extended around the room. People have mixed feelings about cops. Not about firefighters. Community heroes don't need "community relations."

Policemen and firefighters can't strike. The Boston Police Strike of 1919 settled that. "There is no right to strike against the public safety by anybody, anywhere, any time," Governor Calvin Coolidge declared. He called out the National Guard to police the lawless streets and fired the striking cops.

Police and firefighters can't strike, but they can act like strikers—picketing, demonstrating, leafleting—to sway public opinion and move officials to agree to their demands. Making mayors squirm is smart tactics. In good economic times, mayors tend to yield. In bad times, that often means they'll have to make layoffs in other city departments. Take 2010. To pay for the 19 percent raise (later reduced by the City Council) awarded the firefighters by a state arbitration panel, I laid off 250 workers, closed four libraries, and pulled staff out of community health centers.

The economy runs in cycles. Suppose a mayor is generous to fire in an upswing. Then has to negotiate a new contract with the police in a downswing. Police will demand parity with fire. That is the dilemma I sowed with the firefighters' contract I signed in 2001. Police fell behind fire and stayed there. A decade later, the average patrolman's base pay was $15,000 less than a firefighter's. (Though if you include overtime and details, police earned the same as firefighters.) Police leaped ahead in 2013 when a state arbitration panel awarded them a 25.4 percent raise over six years. To my disappointment, the City Council unanimously approved that unaffordable raise. "We're going to have to brace ourselves for the firefighters," a city councilor said. "They may use the same argument." Right, parity. He should have thought of that before voting yes.

I noticed a difference between the public safety unions on the picket line. Despite their higher pay, firefighters tend to be angrier. Policing is a more stable profession than firefighting. Human nature being what it is, criminals will never be in short supply, and cities will need police to handle them. But with fewer fires, we will need fewer firefighters. Welcome news, but not for them.

Increasingly, firefighters don't fight fires. They respond to emergencies. In 2012, 60 percent of the 72,000 calls received by the BFD were for medical and other emergency services; 8 percent were for fires. Major fires fell from 417 in 1975 to 40 in 2012 — a 90 percent decline. Yet the number of firefighters in Boston declined only 12.5 percent, from 1,600 in the 1980s to 1,400 today.

The national picture is similar. Stricter enforcement of building codes, fireproof construction materials, smoke alarms, sprinkler systems, and the fall in the number of smokers have made cities safer. Of the 30 million calls made to fire departments in 2011, only 1.4 million were fire-related — down 50 percent since 1981. Yet the number of firefighters per capita has not changed in decades. "We've got a small army of firemen out there and no fires," writes one expert.

For its army Boston pays $185 million a year. Money well spent, you say. Reviving a man in cardiac arrest with a defibrillator is as much lifesaving work as rescuing a child from a burning house with a ladder. Somebody has to do it. Agreed. But does it have to be a firefighter?

Because fire stations are spread across the city, firefighters are often the first to arrive at an emergency. But in about a third of calls, as soon as the ambulance shows up, the firefighters turn things over to Emergency Medical Service workers.

Reviewing such evidence, Toronto in 2012 stopped dispatching firefighters to nearly fifty types of medical emergencies they used to respond to along with ambulances. Toronto firefighters claim the public is less safe; but stricken people are not being left to die on the streets. They are being treated by EMS workers. They have the same medical training as firefighters, but their benefits package — wages, health care, pensions — is lighter.

Boston could follow Toronto and free resources from fire to fund education and crime prevention. Or Boston could follow New York and Washington and combine fire and EMS in one department, with fewer fire trucks and more ambulances.

Big change like that awaits Boston's next fiscal crisis, when necessity may force decision. But to any future mayor seeking to adjust the ratio of firefighters to fires, good luck. You'll need it.

The firefighters' union fought me at every turn, and usually won. Firefighters were always admired, but 9/11 made them national icons. I was mayor during two recessions, and I laid off hundreds of city workers. But I didn't dare touch the BFD's budget. The issue was never how much to cut but how much more to spend.

More progress was made in changing the culture of the firehouse. The St. Clair Commission of the Fire Department was the O'Toole Commission. I accepted salary increases higher than the city could afford, and the Fire Department accepted more women and minority firefighters. I traded money for diversity.

150 YEARS UNIMPEDED BY PROGRESS. So boasted a banner carried by Chicago firefighters. It could be the motto of the Boston Fire Department. Listen to what a young firefighter told the O'Toole Commission: "Tradition is an anchor around our necks. Our fear of change is killing us."

In a department with roots in the eighteenth century, tradition dictated that firefighters were men. So in 2000, out of a force of 1,592 there were twelve women firefighters (something I called "outrageous"). None of the twelve held rank. When, in a deposition before the Massachusetts Commission Against Discrimination, a district fire chief was asked why he had not promoted a qualified female firefighter, he replied, "Because people didn't like her, and I think it should be a man's job."

Some of the twelve women firefighters were treated well. Others were not. A woman assigned to the East Boston firehouse testified that her pillow was urinated on, marijuana was planted in her fire coat pocket, and she was physically threatened. When her fire gloves were stolen, she protested to her superior. He took action, telling his men to cut it out. For this, he said in a discrimination suit, headquarters ordered him to see a psychiatrist.

Tradition dictated that the Boston Fire Department was an exclusive club for Irish American men who rode fire engines with shamrocks on the doors. So in 2000, the percentage of minorities selected as superior officers stood at 3 percent. In Paul Evans's Police Department, five times more minorities held rank.

Following a wave of lawsuits against the BFD triggered by media exposés, I appointed a special commission of officials and academics led by former state public safety secretary Kathleen O'Toole, one of the four finalists on my list for police commissioner in 1994. Its fifty-eight-page report called for "radical changes to the command structure, promotional system, and department culture."

The O'Toole Commission made sixty-six recommendations, many aimed at easing gender and racial tensions. Some I could introduce myself. Others — curbing abuses in sick leave, ending the practice of working twenty-four-hour shifts, and introducing drug testing — had to be negotiated with the union.

After negotiations stalled in December 2000, the firefighters turned up the heat. They demonstrated at my Christmas tree lighting ceremony, picketed me at a National League of Cities conference in Boston, and slapped a GRINCH bumper sticker on my Ford

Expedition. Then came an X-rated shout-fest at my State of the City address in January.

People arriving at John Hancock Hall were met by 2,200 picketers, including firefighters from across the state. A flying wedge of helmeted cops led my family and me through a side door. The crowd shouted "Shame on you!" and goons spat on Angela. My parks commissioner, Justine Liff, and a group of her co-workers got the same treatment.

"I've been around a long, long time, and never do I remember anything like this happening," remarked former city councilor Richard Iannella. "This is the mayor's address to the people. In my view it's shameful."

The union had put out the word to boycott the speech. We were afraid of rows of empty seats showing up on the eleven o'clock news. So we packed the hall with rank-and-file city workers. From their applause you'd think their jobs depended on it.

I never had any trouble with protesting police but nearly squared off with an angry firefighter. It happened in a Dorchester playground and of all things at a coffee hour for mothers. The guy wagged a finger in my face and told me what I could do with my contract. I was about to forget myself when a mom pushed in between us, put a finger in *his* face, and lit into him. I treasure the memory: The feisty mom was my daughter Susan.

The city offered a 13.8 percent pay raise over three years. The union held out for 20 percent. But the real stumbling block was one of the O'Toole recommendations.

The union fought to preserve a perk singled out by the commission: Because a grateful Commonwealth exempted them from paying state income taxes, injured firefighters on leave were paid more than their regular salaries. Injuries in the BFD were three times higher than in the BPD. A cynic—or an economist—might conclude that firefighters had an incentive to be injured. Boston taxpayers paid twice as much per capita for fire protection as taxpayers in Philadelphia, Los Angeles, or Minneapolis. High injury rates were a big reason why.

I wanted (1) independent medical examiners to assess firefighters' capacity to return to work, and (2) management to be able to assign light duty to firefighters coming off injuries.

This demand, along with requirements to hire more women and promote more minorities, seemed fair to me. Not to the city councilors who boycotted my speech. Councilor Peggy Davis-Mullen spoke for them when she told reporters that what the firefighters wanted, they deserved to get.

They got a raise and the city won some concessions on the O'Toole issues. The terms of the contract were agreed to in the last days of August 2001. Two weeks before 9/11.

I lucked out on the timing. After 9/11, I couldn't have denied anything to our firefighters—not with Boston's firehouses draped in black bunting for their 340 New York colleagues killed at the Twin Towers. And especially in an election year. Davis-Mullen was my opponent. She'd hoped to exploit the union's anger at me over the contract. Settling the contract settled her fate.

QUESTION FROM A REPORTER: Is it true, Mayor Menino, that you slammed down the phone on John Kerry Saturday?
ANSWER: I did not. . . . Not on Saturday.

I'd had labor trouble with police. I'd had labor trouble with firefighters. But not at the same time. The year 2004 brought a perfect storm: trouble with police *and* fire. At the worst possible moment:

when Boston was hosting the Democratic National Convention (DNC), with a Boston resident, Senator John F. Kerry, as the party's presidential nominee.

The police union was threatening to picket the convention site, the FleetCenter, home of the Celtics and Bruins. And delegations from big states like California and Ohio put me on notice: They would not cross a picket line.

The convention was Boston's chance to shine in the national spotlight. It was my chance, before an audience of fifteen thousand journalists, to show my stuff as a *Governing* magazine "Mayor of the Year," the "urban mechanic" with his wrench on the nuts and bolts of making things work.

Now, in June, a month before the convention, things weren't working. I couldn't turn on the radio without hearing my competence mocked in a Harry and Louise ad, "Cake," paid for by the police union.

FEMALE VOICE: It's only a month away, and it seems this DNC is going to be the mayor's big party. I sure hope Menino is fixing all the problems.

MALE VOICE: I don't know. There's gonna be the usual protesters, I'm sure, but now it seems that even our city workers will be protesting. With thousands of city workers still without contracts, it doesn't seem like Menino has things under control at all.

FEMALE: He says he's a friend of labor, but what I don't understand is that he hasn't signed a contract with our police in close to three years. . . . [I]t seems that he's not only insulting labor, but threatening our public safety.

MALE: . . . Why on earth pick a fight with the cops when he's got every Democrat in the world looking over his shoulder?

FEMALE: Makes no sense to me, but one thing's for sure: If Menino doesn't get his act together, the whole world will know about it.

MALE: It's the Democrats' party, but when it comes to mismanagement, Menino takes the cake.

I had to keep reminding myself what an achievement it was for Boston, a Democratic city in a blue state, to land the convention. Denver and Orlando, the other finalists, were in swing states.

So how did we do it? By wowing the DNC. Denver and Orlando wined and dined DNC members, but I got Filene's Basement to open at seven A.M. so they could hunt bargains in private. Denver and Orlando gave nifty PowerPoint presentations, but Boston installed a small ice-skating rink in a Los Angeles hotel lobby so California Democrats could cut figure eights under the palm trees. Colorado and Florida had influential Democratic politicians making the case for their cities. But Boston had Ted Kennedy asking the DNC to crown decades of service to his party with a convention in his hometown. What Democrat could refuse the last Kennedy brother?

Ted had two secret weapons. He trotted them out at a key meeting held at the Shoreham Hotel in Washington. Picture a long table with party chair Terry McAuliffe at one end and me at the other . . . But people aren't the point of this scene. Focus instead on the food: the plates of donuts, bagels, and muffins. Suddenly, the doors swing open and Teddy barrels into the room behind Sonny and Splash, his Portuguese water dogs. Splash leaps onto the table, Sonny follows. Watch the muffins disappear, the bagels scatter. Hear the whoops of laughter . . . Denver and Orlando didn't have a chance.

That memory warmed me as the July date of the convention approached and the police union refused to submit to state arbitration. "Our raises are paying for Tom's party," Tom Nee said. I said: "When I had the money I gave them good contracts. I just can't spend money we don't have." State aid to the city had been sharply cut.

June began and ended with trouble from the least likely person in the world.

But first the Secret Service shut down Boston. The Madrid train bombings in March raised fears of terrorism disrupting the first national political convention held since 9/11. The security gods decreed that North Station, a commuter rail hub that shared a building with the FleetCenter, be shut down for a week and ordered forty miles of roads closed, including I-93, the main north-south route through the city, and the tunnels connecting it with Logan Airport. For four days, Boston would be stoppered.

Commuters and employers were livid. Menino! You promised the convention would bring money to the city, not subtract millions from the local economy! "If Democrats really cared about the people who live and work in Boston, they would do us all a favor and stay home." That opinion, from a letter to the editor, was the water cooler talk of the city.

My team was still reeling from the security shutdown when John Kerry dropped his first bombshell: He might not accept the nomination at the convention. Once nominated, he was subject to federal spending limits. President George W. Bush would not be renominated until early September, allowing him five weeks of unlimited spending. Kerry wanted to level the playing field.

Thousands of people had devoted eighteen months of planning to the convention.

Sitting together around the big conference table at the Parkman House, Ted Kennedy and I went hoarse raising $50 million from wealthy Boston boosters to pay for convention-related activities. Teddy played the bad cop. "I want a million dollars," he said to one of the richest men in the world. A few seconds later he hung up the phone. He shook his head. "Do you know what he said? 'I haven't any loose change to give you.' Can you imagine that son of a bitch? I mean, loose change!"

I'd formed Boston 2004, Inc., a nonprofit agency, to prepare the city for the big event, and assigned my deputy chief of staff, Julie Burns, to run it. She'd recruited 13,000 volunteers to squire 35,000 visitors to 1,000 events. And that was just the beginning.

Julie had cleared away every obstacle to a super convention climaxed by the candidate's statement "I accept your nomination for president of the United States" and his campaign-opening acceptance speech. Now, Kerry seemed ready to blow all that off. To drain the buzz from his own convention.

Someone must have seen the smoke rising from Terry McAuliffe's ears, and Kerry Central had second thoughts about Kerry's second thoughts. After all, John Kerry was for accepting the nomination at the convention before he was against it.

I had three weeks to recover before Kerry dropped his second bombshell.

I was hosting the annual meeting of the U.S. Conference of Mayors. I had invited Kerry to address the mayors. He'd promised to come and deliver a major speech on America's unfinished urban agenda. Over the last weekend in June, while mayors attending events ran the gauntlet of picketers shouting "Don't go in!" and I was being greeted everywhere by choruses of "Tom-my, Tom-my, liar, liar!" (because I had a secret pot of money squirreled away), the candidate was having second thoughts about speaking to the mayors on Monday.

"The Boston event is off. He won't cross a picket line," a Kerry spokesman said on Sunday. "No one has informed the mayor that Senator Kerry is not coming," *my* spokesman told a puzzled press. Hours later, the same Kerry spokesman had second thoughts, emailing reporters, "We have not made any official or final decisions."

"Kerry must start out every morning eating waffles," Brian McGrory commented in the *Globe*. "He'd have a tough time distinguishing between heaven and hell. ('Would it be too cold up there?')"

"Everyone makes his own political decisions," I told reporters. "I think Kerry has to make his decision, and I have to make my decision."

Kerry's decision was to cancel on the mayors to appease the unions. When he told me Sunday night, I hung up on him.

My decision was to invite a prominent Massachusetts politician to replace Kerry. Not Ted Kennedy; no fool, weeks earlier he'd begged off speaking to the mayors. But the state's leading Republican.

Governor Mitt Romney won cheers from America's mayors when he said: "I wanted to indicate my support of Mayor Menino. He's a man of courage and integrity. In the executive, you put the people first and not the pickets. . . . Senators don't have to balance budgets. Senators don't have to make those kinds of trade-offs. That's what the mayor has to do, and that's why I want to be here for him." And the mayors gave Romney a standing ovation when he called me "a good Democrat."

"To be called a good Democrat by a Republican — that's great. That shows respect," I said in an interview with the *New York Times*. "Some of the mayors here are disappointed, frustrated, angered by Kerry not showing up. It's all about respect for the mayors, and there was no respect for the mayors. . . . John Kerry will have to live by this decision."

"Oh my. Forget Bush vs. Kerry," McGrory wrote. "The battle of Boston [Menino versus Kerry] has proven a far better show."

In fairness, Kerry was in a bind. He might have crossed a police union picket line—nationally, the union was Republican-friendly. But firefighters were also picketing over their unsigned contract. And early in his campaign for the nomination, the national firefighters' union had endorsed Kerry. He played up having America's heroes on his side, singling out firefighters wearing gold and black KERRY FOR PRESIDENT T-shirts at campaign events. When, days before Kerry was scheduled to address the mayors, the president of the International Association of Fire Fighters asked him not to cross the picket line in Boston, how could he turn them down?

But it's not like that picket line was in front of a sweatshop, I argued to Kerry Central. It was an informational picket. Moreover, independent voters might reward the candidate for refusing to bow to a Democratic interest group. Defying the unions could be John Kerry's "Sister Souljah moment."

No one listened, because the campaign and the unions had made a deal, at my expense.

In early June, the Kerry campaign and the DNC panicked when aggressive picketers prevented tradesmen from entering the FleetCenter. Refitting the arena for the convention all but stopped for three days and only started when I asked a federal court to dispatch U.S. marshals to police the police pickets. The DNC's nightmare—a convention closed by a labor dispute—seemed all too likely. So Kerry agreed to the unions' demand to humiliate me before the mayors; and in return, the unions promised not to humiliate him before the world.

Events eclipsed the deal. The police union finally agreed to arbitration, and twenty-four hours before the convention opened, a state arbitrator awarded the police 14.5 percent and firefighters 10.5 percent raises over four years.

That was bad news for Boston's taxpayers. The firefighters celebrated at Dorchester's Florian Hall. "As the party got underway," a reporter noted, "firefighters carried stacks of picket signs from the parking lot, to be stored in the office for later use." The signs would come out again in a few years. The ruling set a precedent: Even in a down economy, the public safety unions could expect healthy raises from a state arbitration panel. Police and fire have no incentive to negotiate voluntarily with the city. Arbitrators will always give them more.

But the settlement was good news for the Democrats. The convention would go smoothly. And the city looked great, with baskets of flowers hanging from new street lanterns.

"Beyond the drama, Menino is doing what he does best, the nuts and bolts work of running the town," McGrory wrote. The urban mechanic was back on the job.

We've Hit a New Low in Depravity

— a headline about the Mattapan murders of September 2010

As the years passed, America's cities suffered the unintended consequences of the Politician Preservation Act of 1994, better known as the crime bill. Its $23 billion built a lot of prisons. Its mandatory minimum sentences filled the prisons with a lot of drug felons. They served eight or ten years, then, starting in 2005–6, began leaving. They may not have been violent criminals when they went in, but many turned violent after they came out. Police noticed their presence in the streets right away. Mini–crime waves could be traced to the release of particular inmates. In prison young men survived by "fronting"— that is, violently confronting any inmate who disrespected them. To let anything pass showed weakness. Weakness invited rape. That was the brutal world created by the crime bill. And the young men brought it home with them.

The Mattapan murderers were such young men. The headline about their crime did not exaggerate. I was in New York when Boston hit this new low in depravity. I caught the first flight out and went directly from Logan Airport to Mattapan.

I walked up Sutton Street and began knocking on doors. People needed to see I cared, the city cared, and to hear from me how *they* could secure their streets. A new program run out of community health centers, Violence Intervention and Prevention, mobilized citizens to fight crime. I told them they weren't helpless. Together, they were strong.

The people I met were in shock, and not from finding the mayor on the doorstep. I clasped hands, squeezed shoulders, and listened. They had seen awful things, and wanted me to understand.

Just after one A.M. on September 28 they were awakened by gunfire. "Dad, is it the Fourth of July?" a six-year-old asked his father, who ran outside to investigate. "After what I saw, I plan on moving and going somewhere else," he said. In a vacant lot beside a house on Woolson Street were the bodies of two men, both naked. Police found a third man, barely alive, in bushes nearby. The neighbors were trying to cleanse their eyes of that horror when the bodies of a young mother and her son were carried past them on stretchers. The boy made a small bundle under the blanket. Amani Smith was two years old.

I turned the corner onto Woolson. In front of the house of death was a little shrine made of pink roses, a red balloon, and two teddy bears.

Later, speaking at police headquarters, I addressed the killers, still at large: "To those who have no respect for life and would commit this brutal act, I say this: Our streets are not your battleground. Our kids cannot be your collateral damage. We will not allow you to poison our city."

My emotions were still raw from an atrocity three weeks earlier: the murder of a pizza delivery man making a late-night stop. Richel Nova's death touched me personally. It happened in Hyde Park, my old neighborhood. Two teenagers and a twenty-year-old broke into a vacant house on Hyde Park Avenue, my street. One of them, an eighteen-year-old Hyde Park High student, called Domino's Pizza for a delivery. She called again a few minutes later, impatient.

A security camera on the garage across the street shows Nova's Subaru pulling up in front of the house at 11:30. The camera records the girl walking down the driveway to meet him. According to police, she told him she'd left her wallet inside and to follow her to the back door to be paid. On the garage video they disappear. Seconds later the girl and her two accomplices are seen hurrying down the driveway. They get into the Subaru and drive away.

A police officer who viewed the tape said it was "like watching a horror movie where you want to shout out, 'Don't follow her!' " The two men were waiting for Nova inside the back door. They stabbed him and robbed him of $100. And took the pizza. Coming down the driveway the second time, the girl is holding the box.

A symbol of the New Bostonians renewing the city, Richel Nova was a fifty-eight-year-old Dominican immigrant who worked twelve hours a day, six days a week, putting twin daughters through college. Michelle and Marlene were summer interns at City Hall during the four years they attended Boston Latin, the city's premier high school. I knew them well. "They loved their father so much," I told reporters.

At the funeral, as the front rows formed up behind the coffin, first Richel's widow, Marilin, was overcome, and then one of the twins, and on the procession up the aisle I had to steady mother and daughter.

Meeting with Emerson College students, I was asked whether the killers should get the death penalty. I gave my standard answer—that I don't support the death penalty because it unfairly targets the poor. Then I remembered how Richel was killed—stabbed sixteen times and his throat slit. And I lost it. "If I saw these guys in a dark alley," I said, "I'd like to have a fight with them. I'd do something that would be worse than the death penalty. . . . Because it wouldn't happen in a second. . . . I would slowly torture them."

I instantly regretted it. And apologized on TV. Anger and fear don't belong in public life. Citizens can say what they feel; officials can't afford the luxury.

I was careful not to speak what I felt about the suspects in the Mattapan murders. Two of them met in prison, the school of violent crime. Despite their criminal records, they had obtained semiautomatic pistols. One of the three, thirty-four-year-old Dwayne Moore, knew drugs were being sold from an apartment on Sutton Street. They got a modest haul—a safe, a television, some drugs, and $1,800 in cash—from the three men and one woman in the apartment. They stripped the men, to discourage them from running for help. Then they marched the naked men and the woman, carrying her son, into the vacant lot, made them lie facedown on the ground, and executed them.

Moore was the shooter. He'd spent half his life behind bars. He didn't want to go back. Maybe that's why he killed the four adults—they were witnesses. But the child? Friends described Moore as a hard man dragging a hard life behind him. When his mother came to Boston for his trial, she stayed in a homeless shelter. A hard life. It had made him a monster.

About a third of murders in Boston are retaliatory. A member of Gang A shoots a member of Gang B, and in retaliation a member of B shoots a member of A. There's the contagion of violence, and there's the gun. I mounted initiatives to address both.

One was in public health.

What moved me to adopt that approach to violence prevention was a gang shooting. A mother who witnessed it was courageous enough to tell the police what she saw. I wanted to thank her for helping get the bad guys off our streets. She came to my office, her young kids in tow. I asked what they did after school, and she said, "Nothing." She was afraid to let them play outside. I thought, *No way, not in my city.* That afternoon, I told my team we had to come at the neighborhood-killing problem of youth violence in a new way.

Boston's Violence Intervention and Prevention (VIP) program is a comprehensive strategy to strengthen communities to resist the epidemic of kids shooting kids. VIP volunteers knock on doors in high-risk areas. Ask people about their concerns. Give out numbers to call for help with jobs, rent, mental health, immigration issues, schools, and crime. Youth development specialists instruct kids in conflict resolution and peer leadership skills. Public Health Commission educators assigned to community centers run parent-support workshops. As part of VIP, the schools teach a K–8 violence prevention curriculum named for Louis Brown, the fifteen-year-old honor roll student who was my first dead kid as mayor. And Neighborhood Peace Councils bring together police, residents, clergy, and representatives of city agencies. The Peace Councils make public safety a shared responsibility, though in some neighborhoods apathy limits their effectiveness in preventing violence.

Not apathy but fear sustained violence in "Bowdoin-Geneva," a sixty-eight-block patch of Dorchester where shootings were four times the rate for the city as a whole. It wasn't only that gangs intimidated residents from identifying shooters. Gang values had taken hold in Bowdoin-Geneva. Forty-one percent of residents in one survey believed violence was a justified response to insults.

Police classified Bowdoin-Geneva as a violence "hot spot," and Hendry Street off Bowdoin as a "red zone." Only 570 feet long, this dead end was the most violent street in the city and the street hardest hit by the foreclosure wave of 2007–8. Of its twenty dwellings, ten were in foreclosure, most were abandoned, several were overrun by squatters, and tenants in the multifamily house at the end of the street were dealing drugs.

In disaster I saw opportunity. A chance to foreclose on Hendry Street's violent past.

In early 2008, dozens of city workers converged on the street. They towed away derelict cars, installed new streetlights, swept up trash, planted trees, and put up a new street sign. Standing before a poster announcing THE HENDRY STREET PROJECT, I proclaimed "a new start for Hendry Street." Its derelict condition made three-family houses purchasable for as little as $24,000. The city's Foreclosure Intervention Team* bought four, a local nonprofit four more. We sold them to a local developer, who rehabbed them. The PBS home improvement show *This Old House* filmed some of the work. By 2010 the houses were selling for $250,000, a sum affordable for first-time buyers, who could live in one unit of the three-deckers

* Foreclosure Intervention Teams case-managed every notice of foreclosure that appeared in city or neighborhood papers. At Northeastern University's Reggie Lewis Center, we brought together people in danger of losing their homes with representatives of the banks that held their mortgages. In "work-out" sessions, deals were struck between home owners and lenders. Not all homes were saved. But many were. And our activist approach was adopted by other cities. With Washington blocking a national solution to the wave of foreclosures, we could not sit back and do nothing while good people were thrown out on the street because of the financial crisis.

and rent out the other two. I declared victory: "Families can once again call this place home."

But the big house at the end of the street still harbored dealers, the nucleus of a local gang. After a rival gang sprayed bullets into a backyard Fourth of July cookout in 2010, wounding two gang members and two women bystanders, I ordered a patrol car parked on Hendry Street around the clock. That stopped the shootings; the dealers, who avoided arrest by peddling their drugs elsewhere, remained. I promised residents to keep the car on Hendry for a year. After that, I knew the dealers' rivals would attack again, beginning a new cycle of retaliatory violence.

The dealers were legal tenants. To drive them out, we hit on the idea of condemning the building. The public health approach to crime prevention. In December 2012 a team of twenty inspectors converged on the big yellow house. They encountered a pit bull on one porch and spotted a half dozen other dog cages on balconies and side porches. And ran for their lives. A hurry-up call went out to the city dog officers. The inspectors tried again. In the basement they found what they were looking for: rat droppings, faulty wiring, rusted-out exhaust pipes on the furnace. The house was a health hazard. Everybody was ordered out immediately. A blue NO TRESPASSING sign with my name on it was nail-gunned into the front door.

In 2008 Hendry Street was tenanted mostly by squatters. Now owners occupy just about every house. They have a stake in the street, a financial incentive to help them overcome their fear of helping the police collar the bad guys.

Dr. Barbara Ferrer, my public health commissioner, framed the challenge of violence prevention this way: "It's really about getting the community to feel like they have an essential role in building peace in the neighborhood. It's about creating a culture of peace."

• • •

The other initiative was in national politics.

In 1995, the first year of the "Boston miracle," John Rosenthal, founder of Stop Handgun Violence, erected a huge billboard beside the Massachusetts Turnpike in Boston showing photographs of people shot to death. Since the billboard went up, more than 600,000 Americans have died by the gun.

I once asked a fifth-grade class at one of the city's best charter schools, How many of you know someone with a gun? Over half raised their hands. The headmaster almost had a nervous breakdown. Fifth-graders.

Massachusetts has strict gun control laws. But more than 60 percent of the illegal guns seized in Boston, like the one that killed Officer Wayne Anderson, come from out of state. There's a flourishing interstate commerce in gun murder. Only federal action can stop it.

Yet after a gunman with an assault rifle massacred twenty children in Newtown, Connecticut, in 2012, and with 90 percent of Americans demanding action, the Democratic Senate could not pass universal background checks. The Republican House did not so much as hold a subcommittee hearing on guns.

In 2006 New York Mayor Mike Bloomberg and I started Mayors Against Illegal Guns. We began with fifteen members; today MAIG includes over one thousand mayors, representing 56 million Americans. We're the people's lobby for safe streets. Our goal is not gun control but crime control.

After national legislation died on Capitol Hill, MAIG outlined an ambitious agenda to hire fifty professionals to take the fight to state legislatures in Nevada, Oregon, Colorado, Maryland, Delaware, and Connecticut. I asked Mike Bloomberg where we'd get the money for that. Don't worry about the money, he said.

If a slaughter of six-year-olds won't move politicians cowed by the gun lobby, maybe Bloomberg's millions will. For the first time in decades, the National Rifle Association is on the defensive. Already MAIG has run ads attacking NRA-cozy senators of both parties. More ads will follow against more senators who stood with the NRA against America.

Let's be real. The only language senators understand is money. The only message certain to get through to them is defeat. Democrat or Republican, some have to be driven from office as an example to the others. Then votes will change, and kids and cops now under the gun will live.

A CITY FOR ALL

> St. Patrick's Day is a day when the Irish-American community swells to embrace everyone.
>
> —*Mary Robinson, Ireland's president, during her visit to Boston, March 11, 1994*

I was among the first elected officials in the country to endorse gay marriage. The political wise guys said I was taking a big chance: Boston is a heavily Catholic city. So I conducted a focus group with Frankie, a neighbor who runs a garage:

ME: *What do you think about this same-sex marriage?*
FRANKIE: *If they want to be miserable, let 'em do it.*

I knew I was safe after that.

I was mayor of all the people.

That included Boston's newest residents, the immigrants from Europe, Africa, Asia, and Latin America who, with so much else, have changed the tastes of a city where London broil was once considered an exotic import. My mother's son, I set up a special office to help these New Americans.

All the people included Boston's women. I appointed Boston's first woman police commissioner, first woman corporation counsel, first woman director of the Boston Redevelopment Authority (BRA), first woman mayoral campaign manager, and first woman chief of staff to the mayor. Under my administration, all city employees were given four paid hours off each year for cancer screening. When my public health commissioner told me how many African American women suffered from breast cancer, we fitted out a van to conduct mammograms and parked it in front of beauty parlors in minority neighborhoods. Thousands of women gained years of life from preventive care.

In my last State of the City address I outlined a plan to make Boston the "premier city for working women in the country." A citywide conversation began about increasing workplace opportunity for women. Fifty employers representing 130,000 employees signed the Boston Women's Compact, pledging to achieve pay equity for women. My use of the bully pulpit influenced President Barack Obama's call to employers to pay men and women equally for the same work.

I also defended abortion rights for women. The Church disapproved. At the funeral for former mayor Kevin White, word came down from the hierarchy: Menino can't speak from the altar during the Mass.

I could expand on what we did for immigrants and women. But my record would not be so different from other big-city mayors'.

On gay rights, I made a historic difference. See if you don't agree.

Growing up in Hyde Park, I heard the slurs for "homosexual" but never the word itself.

Harry Collings was the first gay man I met. We worked together at the BRA. He is a good-looking guy, and some of the women in the office, curious why he hadn't asked them out, peppered me with Harry questions. I didn't want them to feel rejected, but I couldn't reveal his secret. So I hinted he had a girlfriend and left it at that.

As a city councilor in the 1980s, I held hearings on needle exchanges to contain the AIDS epidemic. I wanted to know if the rate of infection among addicts was falling in cities that were handing out clean needles in exchange for used ones. To find out, I commissioned two researchers at Harvard's Kennedy School of Government, double-degree candidates in medicine and government, to study exchange programs in cities like New Orleans. Their recommendation that Boston set up a needle exchange was accepted by Mayor Ray Flynn, who claimed the idea as his own. As mayor, I wasn't eager to share credit either.

In my time in office I lobbied a conservative speaker of the Massachusetts House to pass a bill extending to the partners of gay city employees the same health benefits as the spouses of their straight co-workers. I came out for civil unions when it was still considered politically risky. When I endorsed gay adoptions, the Cardinal boycotted a Catholic Charities dinner honoring me. The controversy boosted ticket sales. Right-wing protesters shouted endearments as I entered the hall. My staff printed up hundreds of cards inscribed with the corporal works of mercy and put one on every plate. Haven't read them lately? Consider number seven. By adopting kids who would otherwise grow up in foster homes, weren't gay couples "harboring the harborless"?

Chick-fil-A wanted to come to Boston. What did I think of that? a reporter asked. Not much, I said. The owner, Dan T. Cathy, had contributed nearly $2 million to anti–gay rights groups. I didn't want his business in my city.

The ACLU slammed me: I couldn't ban a business for the owner's *political opinions. No, but the ruckus I raised scared Chick-fil-A away from opening a franchise in Boston. Months after everybody had forgotten about Chick-fil-A, I got a note from Mr. Cathy asking me to give the enclosed to the Perkins School for the Blind, one of my favorite local charities. It was a check for $500,000.*

Gays did not have to travel beyond the city limits to find people who agreed with Dan Cathy. Some of those opponents of equal rights ran the St. Patrick's Day parade held in South Boston since 1901. The holiday celebrated on March 17 is a day for the Irish behind the beard of Evacuation Day, when George Washington, with cannon placed in Southie, drove the British out of Boston.

Fidel Castro was once invited to march in the St. Patrick's Day parade, but aside from that and the usual public drunkenness, the parade stayed out of trouble until 1992, when the organizers told gays they could not march.

The gays were in good company. In 1946 Charlie MacGillivary was rejected when he ran for chief marshal of the parade, and he was a Medal of Honor winner. Charlie was born in Canada: The South Boston Citizens' Association didn't want any damn Canuck leading their parade. Not even one who had lost an arm fighting for the USA.

Veterans protested Charlie's treatment to Mayor Curley, who ruled that from then on, the parade's sponsor would be the South Boston Allied War Veterans Council.

This was the outfit that, in 1992, banned the Irish-American Gay, Lesbian, and Bisexual Pride Committee from their parade. The gay leaders "would not guarantee they would act in a decent way," said a parade committee official, John "Wacko" Hurley. "We didn't know what they would be up to during the march."

After the gays promised the police in writing not to throw condoms at Catholics or commit other outrages, Mayor Ray Flynn said that settled the public safety issue. He called on the vets to let the twenty-five-member gay group march. I was a city councilor then, and I supported the right of gay Irish Americans to join a parade honoring Irish America.

A week before the parade, the gays filed a lawsuit against the Veterans Council, the city, and the mayor. The city because it contributed $8,000 to pay for marching bands and allowed parade organizers to use the city seal on their stationery. A Suffolk Superior Court judge, Hiller Zobel, ruled that the gays had a right to march.

"The Court is satisfied, the marchers are satisfied, and the people of South Boston are satisfied," declared Mayor Flynn, who lived in South Boston. He predicted a "safe, peaceful, fun family day." He wished he could join in, but on the day of the parade he'd be in Northern Ireland, where, he joked, he'd feel "safer" than in Boston.

For the twenty-five gay marchers, that was no joke. They endured a "near-relentless storm of abuse," the Globe *reported. "For the entire length of the parade, attended by an estimated 600,000 spectators, scores of youths surged down sidewalks in pursuit of gay marchers, sometimes urged on by older spectators yelling 'get them.'" People shouted, "We hate you!" and "Hope you die of AIDS!" They turned their backs on the gays. Gave them the finger. A few flung smoke bombs. One marcher was hit in the face by a rock.*

Showing courage, the gays waved and shouted, "Happy Saint Patrick's Day!" Afterward, Barbra Kay, chairwoman of the group, said: "I was really proud to be there. Nothing I heard today was something that I haven't heard before; gay men, lesbians and bisexuals live with harassment every day."

Passing through Dublin, Ray Flynn said, he "picked up the leading newspaper in all of Ireland and the headline was: 'Corridors of

Hatred in Boston.'" Gays had marched in the St. Patrick's Day parade in Cork, where his ancestors were from, and gays would march in Boston: "Were going to have a parade in Boston that is going to be inclusive — open to anyone who wants to abide by the rules. That's the way it's going to be."

Before the 1993 parade, lawyers for the veterans sued to have gay marchers banned. Gays were offensive to the "traditional values" of the parade. To let the gays participate would violate the vets' "freedom of expression."

Judge Zobel again sided with the gays. "The history of the parade shows it to be a secular event," he wrote. He noted the number of non-Irish groups signed up for that year's parade, including a troupe of clowns from New Hampshire, and concluded that the vets "as permit holders, are . . . merely the custodians of a civic tradition."

So gays marched in 1993. But not City Councilor at-Large Albert L. "Dapper" O'Neil. "For the first time in many years," he declared, "I will not be part of the parade, because I will not have my nose rubbed into their way of living." The small band of gays were cursed, spat on, and pelted with snowballs. Vendors sold T-shirts printed with the words 90 YEARS WITH NO QUEERS. *That was the last parade I marched in.*

As mayor in 1994 I tried to bring the two sides together. But when the Supreme Judicial Court found that the gay marchers could not be banned, the vets canceled the parade. "They will never, ever march down the streets of South Boston as a group again," said Wacko.

At the eleventh hour, I tried to persuade other South Boston citizens' groups to sponsor the parade. I got no takers. Finally, I announced a substitute celebration (minus the green beer) at City Hall Plaza and said that, if necessary, the city would sponsor the 1995 parade.

"I'm struck by Menino's willingness to stand up for what he believes

in," said a board member of the Greater Boston Lesbian and Gay Political Alliance. "That's real significant for us. We didn't get that kind of support from Flynn."

Seven times state courts ruled that gays should have "equality of access" to the parade, a "civic celebration." But in January 1995 a federal judge sided with Wacko and the vets, who had come up with a new constitutional angle: Their lawyers made over the St. Patrick's Day parade into a protest march.

"The 1995 parade will protest the decisions of the courts of the Commonwealth," wrote U.S. District Court judge Mark L. Wolf. "Speech addressing such matters is at the core of self-expression that the First Amendment is intended to protect." If the gays marched, "the veterans' protest would be confused and muted; indeed, the veterans' protest would be silenced because they would cancel the parade again."

"In essence, what the judge ruled is that the St. Patrick's Day parade no longer exists," Mary Bonauto, a gay rights lawyer, commented. "The veterans destroyed the parade in order to save it. It is no longer a parade, but an anti-gay protest." Parade officials would wear black armbands, and an opening motorcade would fly black flags.

Wacko Hurley was confident that the U.S. Supreme Court would uphold Judge Wolf's ruling. Regardless, the protest/parade would go on. "If necessary, we'll protest the rest of our lives," he said.

When a group of former servicemen suffering from AIDS applied to march, Wacko turned them down. Asked why, he said: "We don't give reasons. It's our parade." Asked where he got his nickname, he said: "I was born with it. . . . If you find out where it comes from, you let me know."

My office released this statement: "The federal court has ruled very directly on the 1995 parade, ordering the city to give the veterans a permit. The City is now obligated to comply with the judge's ruling and will do so."

"I am not planning to march in the parade," I said. "Many South Boston residents will be attending events which are open to all and I feel my time should be spent with them." One year Angela and I were invited to a St. Patrick's Day reception at the home of Bill Bulger, the veteran South Boston legislator. A burly guy started in on me about the awful gays (only he didn't say "gays"). Bill's wife, Mary, stepped between us and straightened him out: The mayor is a guest in our house. You are way out of line. Please leave now. He did. Occasionally we'd even drop by Wacko Hurley's house party for banter and green bagels. Principled differences—yes. But when politicians read their opponents out of the human race, they give the rest of us a bad example.

My stand on the parade hurt an old pal. "I feel like I've been slapped in the face by a friend," said Jimmy Kelly, Southie's city councilor. "Menino turned his back on an awful lot of good and decent people in order to be politically correct." The papers speculated that my decision not to march "caused a rupture in the mayor's friendship with Kelly." Certainly it made a rift.

I laid down a policy followed for the next two decades. City workers could not participate in the march. City emblems could not be shown. And, except for public safety during it and street cleanup after, city money could not be spent on the parade.

"I am gratified by the mayor's leadership on this issue," said Cathleen Finn, spokeswoman for GLIB, the Irish-American Gay, Lesbian, and Bisexual Group of Boston. "It is clear that anyone who participates in the parade is serving to legitimize discrimination." A Globe *editorial called my ban on on-duty city workers representing Boston at the parade "courageous."*

• • •

June 10, 1995, was the silver anniversary of Boston Gay and Lesbian Pride Day, commemorating the Stonewall Riots in 1969, when police beat gay men resisting arrest at a Greenwich Village bar. Over 100,000 spectators lined the streets of downtown, the South End, and the Back Bay watching—and cheering—thousands of marching gay, lesbian, bisexual, and transgender men and women. Many wore T-shirts reading CLOSETS ARE FOR CLOTHES. *"Times have changed since I first marched in the 70s," one man said. "It is not so much a political event as a celebration. We're out and proud today."*

I was proud that my friend Harry Collings, director of development at the Fenway Community Health Center, was a grand marshal of the parade.

It was Boston's first Dyke March, with a large contingent of lesbians joining the parade in Copley Square. From a stage in front of the Old South Church on Boylston Street, a few hundred feet from where the first bomb exploded in April 2013, I told the marchers: "Twenty-five years of progress and positive change have passed since those brave gay men and lesbians marched up Charles Street in 1970. . . . Your strength in numbers today sends a loud and clear message that every single person in this wonderfully diverse city matters. . . . We all know that the mean-spiritedness must stop."

In 2014, for the twentieth year in a row, Wacko & Co. kept gays from marching in the St. Patrick's Day parade. So the mean-spiritedness hasn't stopped. But it will stop. Gays will march. As the Yiddish saying has it, Where there's mortality, there's hope.

Usually I marched in the Gay Pride parade. But in 2013 I was sidelined by the broken leg that, three days before the Marathon bombing, landed me in the hospital. Angela took my place. Recuperating at the Parkman House, I watched the parade from a wheelchair inside the vestibule. A young woman, spotting me, left the marchers, ran across

Beacon Street, and bounded up the stone steps. She wanted to thank me, she said. Years before, rejected by her parents, she'd left her hometown and come to Boston, a stranger. But, she said, beginning to cry, I'd helped her feel that Boston was her home. She wiped her tears, squeezed my hand, and rejoined the parade. As I battle cancer, her words bring me contentment.

Chapter 4

Getting Stuff Done

> Cities and metropolitan areas are on their own. The cavalry is not coming.
>
> — *from* The Metropolitan Revolution: How Cities and Metros Are Fixing Our Broken Politics and Fragile Economy *by Bruce Katz and Jennifer Bradley*

IN THE new America, cities have to supply their own cavalry. Mayor Mike Bloomberg stated their challenge this way: "As a result of [the federal] leadership vacuum, cities around the country have had to tackle our economic problems largely on our own."

A partisan standoff paralyzed economic policy after the Tea Party won control of the House in the 2010 elections. With millions unemployed, Washington did nothing. Scratch that. To block "Obamacare," the Tea Party shut down the government and threatened to destroy the nation's credit.

Project the Tea Party backward. Suppose those radicals were in office in 2008–9, when the financial crisis morphed into a recession. Almost certainly they would have blocked the policies that prevented "the worst recession since the Great Depression" from turning into a second Great Depression — President George W. Bush's loan program to prop up the tottering banking system and President Barack Obama's $800 billion stimulus to revive the economy.

Now project the Tea Party roadblock forward: In the next recession, the federal cavalry won't be coming to rescue the economy.

That's the situation I faced in 1994. The nation was slowly emerging from recession. Boston was still mired in its worst slump since the 30s, having lost 25,000 good-paying manufacturing jobs in the 80s and 75,000 jobs of all kinds since 1988. The economy needed action, but Washington wouldn't act. In the 1992 election campaign, candidate Bill Clinton promised to restore growth by deficit spending on infrastructure. But after his spending plan bogged down in Congress, President Clinton made deficit reduction his top economic priority. Boston was on its own. "How the public sector can help stimulate economic growth is the crucial question facing the next mayor," said the Reverend Charles Stith, a respected voice of the African American community.

Over the next three years Boston ran an experiment with lessons for post-Washington America: Unable to go into deficit by cutting taxes or increasing spending, the federal cures for recessions, can a city government stimulate prosperity on its own?

Politically, Boston was testing a proposition stated by a local authority on "urban affairs": "Mayors just aren't important anymore." We'd see about that.

The week before the 1993 election, looking back on my months as acting mayor and ahead to my first term, I said: "We have taken positive action in virtually every area of government affecting people's lives. . . . Come November 3rd — the day after you elect me as mayor — the city of Boston will begin a new era in which the needs of families are given the highest priority." Participation in a growing economy was among the highest priorities for Boston families.

"If we can create an economic climate in the city that creates jobs," I said after taking office, "a lot of other problems in the city will take care of themselves."

The mantra of city economic strategy should be: Build it and they will work. Buildings create jobs. Blue-collar jobs in constructing them. White-collar jobs when they are finished.

Consider this: Between 1947 and 1964, only 27,745 jobs in financial and professional services were created in Boston. Between 1964 and 1968, Boston gained 32,000 such jobs. That's more jobs in four years than in the previous seventeen. Something changed in 1964. What? The Prudential Tower, Boston's first skyscraper, was completed. Build it and they will work. (During my tenure, Boston added the equivalent of a new Prudential Tower every other year for a total of 13 million square feet of office space.)

Clinton's turn toward deficit reduction lowered interest rates. That encouraged developers to borrow and build. But they could build anywhere. Why in Boston? I had to show them. How? First, by erasing a question mark over the city's fiscal future. Second, by launching a major project to generate economic activity.

. . . the most important thing I will do as mayor.

—from a City Hall press conference in April 1996

Starting in the 1970s, 128 cash-strapped cities, including Kansas City, St. Louis, Detroit, and Philadelphia, closed their public hospitals. By 2005, 40 percent of the country's remaining public hospitals were predicted to follow them. That wasn't an option in Boston. Not with me as mayor.

Boston City Hospital was a precious social legacy. Established to fight cholera in the nineteenth century, built up to serve the poor by

James Michael Curley in the twentieth century, by the dawn of the twenty-first century BCH was in trouble. To save this great public hospital, I had to privatize it.

To progressives, "privatize" is an ugly word. Government is about helping people, not making money from helping them. That was my belief. Still, to preserve its mission for the new century, I had to risk being remembered as the mayor who sold "the City."

My first month in office I toured the new $170 million Boston City Hospital. It had taken ten years to build and even before admitting its first patient was obsolete. Yet, to pay off its FHA mortgage, Boston was on the hook for $20 million a year for decades. Closing it made no economic sense.

Changing patterns of health care were working against BCH:

- With fewer illnesses requiring hospital stays, hospitals were competing for a shrinking number of patients.
- Competition was intense in Boston, the health care capital of America, where major independent hospitals were merging.
- As they merged, they offered more comprehensive procedures, becoming more attractive to insurers and HMOs competing to offer customers total care.
- Under national health insurance — then "Clintoncare" — instead of being "steered" to public hospitals, the poor would be enrolled in health care plans specifying which hospitals to use. Compared to the merged private hospitals, BCH had little to offer those plans. It would lose its patient base to the private competition.

In March 1994 a commission on the future of BCH recommended merging it with its next-door neighbor in the South End, Boston

University Medical Center Hospital, and that "dramatic reductions be made in costs in order to save the municipal hospital."

How would it work? I asked. No one could tell me. Public hospitals had been shut. Some had been sold. None had been merged with a private hospital. We'd be stepping off into the public policy void. The merger was what I called it — an opportunity for "Boston to make history."

I appointed former state senator Patricia McGovern to lead a second commission to coordinate the merger. "The commission's job is to get the two hospitals to the altar and actually perform the ceremony," the *Globe* commented. "Within two years, and preferably sooner, the hospitals are to consolidate — merge, unite, become one — legally and operationally. . . . Everyone understands that huge difficulties complicate such a drastic move."

"The biggest obstacle to this merger are the unions," I said. BCH was heavily unionized, University Hospital less so. "We have to make [the unions] understand what happens if we can't do the merger. I understand there is fear that jobs will be wiped out. We'll do the best we can to preserve as many jobs as we can. But if we don't do it, we may lose *all* the jobs."

"Market forces dictate the need to merge if the two hospitals are to remain viable," said Sam Tyler, director of the Boston Municipal Research Bureau, an independent budget watchdog. "Either one cannot survive standing alone."

The numbers told the story. BCH admitted 14,000 patients annually and University Hospital 10,000. Only as a single hospital with 24,000 admissions could it compete with Boston hospitals admitting 20,000 to 35,000 patients.

A second obstacle was the difference in the "client groups" served by each institution. Less than 50 percent of the patients at University Hospital were from Boston, compared to 90 percent of BCH patients. Five percent of University Hospital's patients were poor and only 4 percent were uninsured. Many of BCH's patients were poor and 45 percent were uninsured.

Treating patients regardless of their ability to pay, BCH provided half the indigent care in Boston, and a quarter of it in Massachusetts. Would the merged hospital continue that mission? Would it serve Boston residents or suburbanites? The merger's announced purpose was to cut costs, but could that be achieved without cutting services to those needing them the most? Yes, yes, and yes, we answered critics who raised such questions. But with no experience to guide us, how could we be sure?

A third obstacle was the public relations embarrassment that BCH had a $4 million surplus for 1993 while University Hospital showed a $9 million loss. If BCH was doing so well, why merge it with its failing neighbor? The unions pushed that talking point hard. But by the end of the century, BCH was expected to run an operating deficit of up to $7 million. And every 1 percent drop in patients would add another million. That was one of my talking points. After a year of exposure to the arguments, the public was moving toward support of the merger. I'd been mayor long enough for people to take my measure. They trusted me not to sell out the poor.

To survive, hospitals need patients. So when eight Boston community health centers representing 200,000 patients agreed to make the new merged hospital their principal affiliation, it was a huge step forward. We outbid the private hospitals competing for their patients, promising to contribute $6 million to the health centers for "capital improvements." University Hospital was led by Elaine Ullian, a longtime friend. We easily agreed to kick in $3 million each.

The proposed merger had an unexpected dividend: Standard & Poor's awarded Boston its best-ever credit rating. "We thought the highest risk for the city would be to do nothing with City Hospital," an executive from S&P's Boston office explained. "Clearly they are taking steps to avoid being left in a difficult position with no options." The merger was not about constructing new buildings; but acting today to fix tomorrow signaled that my administration was businesslike and development-friendly. Over the next decade the high bond rating helped the city refinance $600 million in debt, saving taxpayers nearly $35 million and lowering borrowing costs for road repairs, new buildings, and other capital improvements.*

So much for the good news of 1995. My commission delivered the bad news: A private corporation had to manage the hospital "to free [it] from civil service rules, city purchasing requirements and much red tape." Otherwise costs could not be contained. BCH's 131-year history as a public institution was over.

It was a "gotcha" moment for the unions, who had been warning that in any merger "the City" would be swallowed up. The signs members carried at demonstrations—KEEP THE PUBLIC IN HEALTH CARE and STOP THE HOSTILE TAKEOVER OF BCH—had a new bite.

The merger required City Council approval. Appearing before the committee considering the merger, I spoke with feeling. "The hos-

* "If there were a trophy for excellence in financial management, Menino would have won it. . . . His administration has been notably cautious in managing taxpayers' money. Rating agencies examine management practices, debt burden, reserves, and liquidity before determining a city's creditworthiness. . . . Boston is on target to fully fund its $2.1 billion pension liability by 2023, seven years ahead of statutory requirement." From a *Boston Globe* editorial, October 26, 2009.

pitals that resist change, that fail to remain competitive . . . simply will not be in operation at the start of the twenty-first century," I told the councilors. "Let's protect our hospitals from that horrible fate. The people who need them deserve better than that."

The unions were lobbying the councilors to reject the merger unless stronger labor protections were written into it. So to win the vote in the council, we had to win over the unions.

Three days of face-to-face talks around the conference table in the brick-walled meeting room of the Parkman House, a converted carriage barn, brought us close to an agreement. The union heads at the table knew the score. The merger would cost jobs — most, but not all, by attrition. But nothing like the nearly four thousand people who stood to lose their jobs if the merger failed. BCH was Boston's largest employer of minorities. They would lose the most jobs.

My chief of staff, David Passafaro, chaired the sessions. From time to time I stopped by to take the temperature of the room. On the third evening it felt chilly. So I put on a show.

I stood up and, with a swinging hand, swept papers and pencils off the table. I yelled, cursed, and grew red in the face. I said I was tired of the pettiness and the bellyaching. Sick of the speeches and the posturing. It was now or never. Then I took off my watch, slapped it on the table in front of Passafaro, and barked in my General Patton voice: "It's nine o'clock. If you don't have a deal in two hours, I'll go on the eleven o'clock news and denounce the holdouts. David, call me when it's done."

I stormed out of the room, through the long hallway, and down the spiral staircase to the front door. David ran after me. He was afraid I had lost it. Hell, no, I said, when he caught up with me at the front door. It was an act. He started up the stairs. "I want that watch back," I said, and slammed the heavy door behind me.

A deal was struck at three A.M. By a vote of 10 to 3, the City Council approved the merger. It added language to the agreement creating a commission to monitor the merged hospital's care for the indigent. Every year the city would convene a public meeting to hold the hospital to that mission.*

I vowed to drive a hard bargain with the merged hospital (now Boston Medical Center) "to make sure the mission stays the same." The city's subsidy to BMC — $56 million over its first five years and $12 million annually after that — gave me leverage.

"The poor, the homeless, children, elders, the uninsured will not go without appropriate health care while I'm mayor," I declared at an April 1996 City Hall press conference announcing that the two hospitals would operationally become one in July. The merger, I said, was "the most important thing I will do as mayor."

Today Boston Medical Center employs nearly six thousand people. Twenty-five percent live in Boston. Forty-five percent are racial or ethnic minorities. Seventy percent are represented by unions. BMC serves 150,000 low-income patients a year, 65 percent from the poorest Boston neighborhoods. I could tick off its awards, praise its researchers, describe its efficient operation — it finished 2012 with a surplus! But what moves me when I think of BMC is its Grow Clinic, a national model for treating children diagnosed with "failure to thrive," a heartbreaking condition associated with malnutrition, poverty, and family stress. The clinic treats two hundred kids at a time. It saves their lives. It gives them a future. Knowing I helped make that possible fills me with pride.

---

* Two individuals I depended on to advise me on the merger were Dick Nesson of Partners HealthCare and Dean John McCarthy of the Harvard Business School. They were the ones I called on continually whenever we reached an impasse.

I spent nearly $1 million on Irish consultants.

—Robert Kraft, owner of the New England Patriots

A historian of bad ideas could trace the "Boston megaplex" to a spring day in 1992 when Massachusetts governor Bill Weld dropped by the Toronto SkyDome, home of baseball's Blue Jays. The tall redhead stood on the pitcher's mound, wound up, and threw an imaginary strike.

"To his companion, state Secretary of Economic Affairs Stephen Tocco," Joan Vennochi reported in the *Boston Globe,* "it seemed the governor was basking in the echo of cheers from countless . . . fans."

Perhaps he dreamed of taking a bow in the first game played in the WeldDome. Why not? Weld's family dated from the founding of the Bay Colony. His name was on a Boston street. It could be on a Massachusetts town. It belonged on a stadium. He was a ruddy-faced sportsman who hunted boar and caught trout, but after his perfect pitch under the SkyDome, it was Weld who was hooked.

Weld's dream harmonized with the ambition of James Orthwein, then the owner of the New England Patriots football team. The Patriots played in suburban Foxboro in a small rented stadium. Orthwein wanted them to play in Boston (where the franchise began in the early 1960s), in a bigger stadium built by the public. But the taxpayers wouldn't pay for a stadium used ten or twelve times a year. So Orthwein came up with some inspired packaging: Attach a stadium to a convention center in a megaplex, and to make it mega-mega, throw in a new baseball park for the Red Sox.

Weld seized on the megaplex: It gave cover to his dome. He proposed a $700 million convention-sports center financed from revenue generated by five casino boats floating in Boston Harbor and by a diversion of revenue from the city's hotel tax.

This was in 1993. I was acting mayor. "I'm against taking any additional revenues from the city of Boston," I said. "We need every penny to provide services to people who live and work in our city." To shift money from the schools, from police and fire and other city services, to spend on a football stadium? Not on my watch.

I tasked the BRA to research the feasibility of a megaplex compared to a stand-alone convention center. The BRA study, which took seven months to complete, found that the "disadvantages of combining the facilities outweigh any advantages."

The pieces pulled in different directions. The football stadium wanted to be on the outskirts of the city near a highway. The convention center wanted to be downtown, near hotels, restaurants, and public transportation. Unlike City Hospital and University Hospital, merging the separate pieces in a megaplex was not cost-effective. Hosting so few games, the stadium would not stimulate enough commerce to pay for itself, and the convention center could not pay for both.

But it could pay for itself.

"Today I challenge the Legislature and the governor to work with me to get the convention facility built," I said in announcing the study. I laugh at myself now for expecting the project to sail through the legislature.

Boston was among the most desirable cities in the country to hold conventions, but was ranked forty-eighth for its ability to host them, below Wichita, Kansas. The Hynes Convention Center in the Back Bay was too small to compete for meetings of major trade and professional groups. A larger state-of-the art facility was a needed public investment.

The BRA selected a twenty-seven-acre site west of C Street in a fading industrial area between South Boston's residential district and Boston Harbor. Building the convention center would displace no houses and only 284 jobs.

Nor would the center present traffic or parking problems for South Boston. Out-of-town conventioneers would arrive and depart by cabs or public transportation from Logan Airport to the north, not through one of the city's densest areas to the south.

The 600,000-square-foot exhibition center would generate an estimated $436 million a year in direct spending and create from seven thousand to twelve thousand jobs, mainly in retail, transportation, and the hospitality industry. The BRA estimated that the convention center would spur the building of an additional three thousand to five thousand hotel rooms, with one person employed for every new room.

There would be service jobs. In the 80s Boston had lost half its manufacturing jobs. They wouldn't be coming back. The new economy was producing low-wage jobs. Compared to my dad's job at the plant, they weren't great. But unlike manufacturing jobs, they couldn't be outsourced to China. Many of those generated by the convention center would go to Boston's new Americans. Think of the Dominican pizza delivery man, working overtime to get his family started in America; think of Richel Nova gunned down in Hyde Park. Thanks to his sacrifices (and to a scholarship fund we set up), both his daughters graduated from college. Ideally, that's how it is with these jobs. Families stand on them, and the next generation moves up.

The convention center's $440 million cost would be financed by an increase in the hotel tax (not a diversion of Boston's portion), a fee on taxi service, and a $2.50 charge on car rentals. These sources would yield $47 million a year, more than enough to meet the debt payment of $37 million.

The convention center was a thrifty engine of economic development. Conventioneers and tourists would pay the taxes and Massachusetts businesses and residents would reap the benefits.

Becoming mayor in a down economy, my challenge was to use the public sector to stimulate growth and employment. The trade journal *Bond Buyer* captured the strategy in a headline: "Boston Is Building Itself Back to Prosperity."

The multibillion-dollar, nearly two-decade-long "Big Dig"—the federally funded depression of Boston's elevated highway and the construction of a new harbor tunnel—was part of that. Less heralded was Boston's five-year $900 million long-term capital investment campaign. The idea was to avoid the feast-or-famine cycle of construction work seen in the 80s. *Bond Buyer* identified me as "one of the architects of the city's capital plan" because I was chair of Ways and Means on the City Council when it was adopted.

"During this recession, we have made a very conscious effort to put people back to work as quickly as possible," I told *Bond Buyer*. "At the same time . . . we are interested in keeping these people employed. Five years ago, we decided that the schools and the hospitals and the community centers in the city were in desperate need of repair." So the city coordinated with Boston's health care and biomedical research sectors to stagger these projects over a span of years. The new construction would provide a steady tempo of work in the building trades, yield permanent jobs in the new facilities built or existing ones expanded, and "further improve the quality of life in the city."

Bond Buyer forecast that "construction projects partially or fully backed by the city . . . will create about 17,000 construction jobs and 18,000 permanent positions." Some would be public jobs. More would be in private hospitals and research labs. "Although the construction of the Central Artery . . . [has] earned the bulk of the local headlines," *Bond Buyer* concluded, "the permanent employment picture produced by some of the smaller projects may end up as the biggest story of this recession."

The key piece of Boston's do-it-yourself recovery strategy was the convention center. It would boost the economy. As important, it would reassure investors, start-ups, and companies looking to relocate that, recession or boom, Boston got stuff done.

Though approved by a special commission stacked with legislators, by late 1995 the megaplex was foundering in the legislature, pulled down by its cost and especially by its location.

The bill proposed a megaplex for South Boston, near my C Street site for the convention center. In that tight-knit, suspicious, and fiercely political neighborhood, the megaplex touched off mega-resistance.

I heard it in the voices of the six hundred people who came out for a megaplex meeting with me and my BRA director, Marisa Largo. Their message was, Don't let our neighborhood be turned into an exit ramp and parking lot for suburban football fans.

"A lot of people out there want to change our neighborhoods for their own self-interest," I said to a large audience at a ribbon cutting in Southie. "We won't let them do that."

The lesson of the West End devastation of the 50s, the "urban renewal" of the 60s, and the "Inner Belt" bulldozer of the early 70s that I saw firsthand was "never again." The people of Boston would not sacrifice their neighborhoods to "development." They would not even give up intangibles like Sunday quiet.

I'd tell developers: Want to build in the neighborhoods? Talk to the neighbors. Convince *them* that change won't harm their quality of life.

• • •

From the sinking megaplex Weld reeled in a stand-alone domed stadium. For $500,000 a year he offered to lease twenty-two acres of state-owned land on the South Boston waterfront to the Pats' new owner, Bob Kraft, a cardboard box millionaire and an intense local sports fan.

In December 1996 Kraft invited state officials, business leaders, and executives from the *Herald* and the *Globe* to a meeting in a space he rented in the basement of BankBoston, a business ally. He walked his visitors through a full-scale replica of one of the luxury boxes he was counting on to pay for the stadium. You can be sure that Kraft made these two points to his guests: (1) that, unprecedented for a National Football League franchise, he planned to finance the stadium himself, and (2) that other cities were offering a "free"—publicly financed—stadium to lure the Pats away from Massachusetts.

Give newspaper barons news and you can expect to read it in the paper. The *Herald* put the BankBoston meeting—and Weld's offer to Kraft—on the front page. Overnight South Boston's politicians mobilized the community against the stand-alone stadium.

To shift public opinion, Kraft mounted a charm offensive. It did not go well.

At one community meeting a South Boston man asked him: "My kids play on the street every day and I will be right in the shadow of the stadium. What do I do about my house, which we've had for two generations?"

"Don't worry, I'll buy your house," Kraft replied, and took his name and phone number.

Kraft had long since fingered me as the chief obstacle to the stadium. He had that right.

"I don't tell Bill Parcells how to coach his team," I said. "Why does someone come in here and tell me how to build our city?"

The stadium would not only disrupt a city neighborhood. It was a distraction. The focus needed to be on jobs, on building our way to prosperity, on the convention center. I hoped Kraft (and Weld) would see that South Boston was hopeless and move on to another site, whether in Boston (I had suggested one) or the suburbs. But instead of caving on the stadium, they fired up sports fans to pressure me to cave. I was a pol more afraid of losing votes in Southie than of losing the Pats to another state.

> Thomas M. Menino is being hammered unmercifully these days for stubbornly trying to block a proposed new stadium for the Patriots. He has been denounced by the local press, the powerful downtown business community, the Governor and, above all, a legion of fans euphoric that their team—once so bad that spectators would put paper bags over their heads as a sign of embarrassment—is now a winner.
>
> —*from "A Classic Boston Brawl Pits Mayor Against New Stadium,"* New York Times, *January 22, 1997*

January 1997 was a cruel month for me. I was blocking a new stadium for the Pats just as the team went on a tear. In a rally held on frozen City Hall Plaza, fifteen thousand Pats-crazy fans drowned out my pep talk with cries of "Stadium, stadium, stadium!"

For the first time in memory, the *Globe* and *Herald* agreed: I was dead wrong on the stadium.

I read that I was a "small-time mayor." That Boston under Menino was "three steps behind Poughkeepsie." That "Menino doesn't have a vision and the neighborhood is parochial."

The *Globe* ran "news" stories that supported the arguments in its editorials. For example, it solicited this warning from a sage at the Atlanta Chamber of Commerce: "You don't want to get into a political battle and run the team out of town because they will go someplace else." Bob Kraft might follow Art Modell. Two years earlier, with his Cleveland Browns recording the second-highest attendance in the league, Modell had moved the team to Baltimore.

That wouldn't happen in Atlanta, the Chamber man told the *Globe*. They knew how to treat a big-league team down there: "When the Falcons said they wanted a new stadium, Georgia shelled out $200 million to keep them in the city."

Yet in Boston, Kraft was ready to spend $200 million of his own money for a stadium, and still Menino said no.

The *Globe* fretted that "the team will move before he moves. . . . Menino is apparently willing to take the risk that Kraft could move the Patriots on his watch if the team is shut out of South Boston."

In an election year, the risk was political. Worst case: Could I win reelection as "the mayor who lost the Pats"? Turn that around. Could a challenger win on that issue?

I liked my odds.

I'd play the suburban card. I stand with Boston residents, I'd declare, my opponent, with suburban fans who want to turn our neighborhoods into their parking lots. People across the city rooted for the Pats, but they also resented the suburbs.

I'd also play the class card.

To pay for his stadium, Kraft planned to sell six thousand executives midfield seats for $6,000 a year for a minimum of ten years. For their $60,000, Kraft's funders would become members of a private year-round club, with a restaurant, bar, and meeting rooms. Selling tickets to high rollers, Kraft displayed a model not of the stadium but of the club, described by the *New York Times* as "testosterone as architecture, all-wood-paneled walls, leather chairs, a marble bar, helmets and footballs resting on shelves."

Kraft's dome — stadium, club, and NFL "pavilion"— was billed as "self-financed." But Kraft was asking government for $65 million in infrastructure improvements. My challenger would answer for that.

You lost the Pats, he'd say. Where do you get off asking taxpayers to subsidize a country club with an ocean view? I'd retort.

I liked my odds, but the Pats weren't making it easy for me.

To reach the Super Bowl on January 26, first they had to win a playoff against the Pittsburgh Steelers on the fifth and then the AFC championship on the twelfth. If the Pats lost to the Steelers, a sportswriter predicted, sports radio would turn to "come down issues" like the future of coach Bill Parcells. "And if they win? Weld [and] Menino . . . might as well resign and give their seats to . . . Parcells and [quarterback Drew] Bledsoe."

They won. Super Bowl fever gripped New England. On the day tickets went on sale in Foxboro for the AFC decider against the Jacksonville Jaguars, 11 million calls flooded Ticketmaster's phones.

In Foxboro that morning, seven thousand fans turned out to buy three thousand tickets. Milling outside the stadium in the January cold, they showed why *Monday Night Football* had refused to broadcast games from Foxboro for fourteen years. In a booze-fueled melee they traded punches with each other and hurled bottles at the police, who arrested ten before dispersing the crowd with only a thousand tickets sold.

My impulse was to pounce: Picture those palookas streaming into South Boston after Pats games, filling the bars, peeing in the streets, groping the women, and infuriating the men. But I held my tongue, hoping fair-minded observers would empathize with Southie residents.

"It's getting to be show time," Bill Weld said, turning up the heat on me. "We have the AFC championship being played here in Massachusetts and what's the host city? The host city is Providence, Rhode Island."

The headline in the *Herald:* "NFL Snubs Hub."

In a slap at Boston (and me), NFL commissioner Paul Tagliabue named Providence, twenty miles down I-95 from Foxboro, the official pregame NFL headquarters.

"I guess Pawtucket was already booked," I quipped.

"Boston has fumbled," Providence Mayor Buddy Cianci crowed. "My feeling is that if you want to get in the game you have to suit up. . . . If Boston can't accommodate [Kraft], Providence will."

"Some cities need a pro sports team to have people look at them," I shot back, "but people want to come to Boston."

Ten thousand fans turned out in the rain to welcome the NFL to its host city for a week. Merchants draped the Pats logo over their windows. A deli made sandwiches named after star players. It had taken 350 years, but for the first time "excitement" and "Providence" appeared in the same sentence.

Kraft's best argument for a new stadium in Boston was that the old one in Foxboro was falling apart. Well, wouldn't you know, in the AFC championship game the stadium lights at Foxboro went out for eleven minutes. The blackout "makes a point," Kraft told sportswriters. "But we didn't plan it."

With a group of friends, I watched the game at my City Hall office. When the lights went out, someone shouted what everyone suspected: "Whatddeedo, Kraft, throw water on a transformer?"

After Otis Smith gathered up a fumble and ran into the end zone for the fourth-quarter touchdown that sent the Patriots to the Super Bowl in New Orleans, I put my head in my hands and groaned, "Two more weeks of this . . ."

"As Super Bowl hoopla intensifies and the eyes of the nation turn toward New England, no seat will be hotter than that occupied by Mayor Thomas M. Menino," the *Globe* wrote. "If the team leaves the city, it won't matter how many good things he does in office. If the Cleveland Patriots are in some future Super Bowl, Menino will always be remembered as the villain who forced the heroes out of our city." Soon after that commentary ran, on a visit to the Franklin Park Zoo, Kobie, the four-hundred-pound gorilla, pelted me with his feces.

My patience was fraying. Especially with Bill Weld. He needed a win. Like Mitt Romney a decade later, Bill Weld saw being governor of Massachusetts as a launching pad to the White House. He'd wanted to be nominated as Bob Dole's running mate in 1996. That hadn't happened. He'd hoped to unseat Senator John Kerry that November. He'd lost by 9 points. Bill had fizzled out; his national political career seemed likely to end before it began. He needed a win. I understood. But his public needling that the Pats would leave the state if I did not budge was hurting me politically. So I unloaded on him in a phone call not for the ears of the nuns at St. Thomas Aquinas. But you can't insult a Weld. Maybe if my family once owned Readville I'd be unflappable too.

He made amends by inviting Angela to sit with his wife, Susan, in the State House gallery during his State of the State address. But he couldn't resist packing the speech with football references. When he declared, "Our commonwealth is bound for glory in the biggest game of all," Democratic lawmakers sat on their hands. So Bill adlibbed, "It gets better, or worse, depending on your perspective." It got worse. Raising his fist, he shouted, "Jambalaya, Go Pats!"

From my point of view the substance of the governor's speech was worse than the tone. David Nyhan's suggested headlines got the gist: "Weld Croaks Convention Center" and "Governor Rules Out Mayor's Key Economic Goal."

"We promised the citizens that we would not raise taxes — ever — for as long as we are on Beacon Hill," Weld boasted. "And we have not raised taxes. And we never will." Not even to help finance a public investment that would stimulate the Massachusetts economy for years to come.

The Democratic speaker of the House, Tom Finneran, was just as stubborn as Weld, but in the other direction. The state could not borrow the whole cost of the convention center. At least half had to come from user fees on conventioneers. "We haven't blinked and we're not going to blink," Finneran declared. "There's going to be an increase in these taxes or fees or there is not going to be a convention center."

Angela had a good time with Mrs. Weld, but I left the State House in low spirits.

They weren't raised any at the rally seeing the Patriots off to New Orleans. The crowd cheered Weld but booed when I was introduced and chanted "Sta-di-um." The players laughed, egging the fans on . . . in my front yard.

I missed going to my first Super Bowl. A kidney stone insisted on being removed. From my hospital bed, I was enjoying the pregame festivities on TV until the camera lingered on a sign displayed by a Holiday Inn near the Superdome. It read WELCOME BUDDY CIANCI, MAYOR OF PATRIOTS' HOME TOWN.

If the Patriots had defeated the Green Bay Packers in the Super Bowl and kept Coach Parcells from jumping to the New York Jets, things might not have gone downhill so fast for Bob Kraft. At least victory would have put the Pats owner and Jonathan Kraft, his son and point person on the stadium, in a better frame of mind.

Six days after the Super Bowl, talking to Charlie Sennott, a respected business reporter, Kraft asked, "What have I done that's so bad here?" He was puzzled by "all the haters in this town, all those who don't want to take risks."

Mitt Romney talked like that during the 2012 GOP primaries. He was a "risk taker," not a "vulture capitalist." Similarly, a story Sennott told about a Kraft venture in Montville, Connecticut, recalls Newt Gingrich's attack ad about "the day Mitt Romney came to town":

> Kraft and his son Jonathan blew into town, promising to create 80 jobs by adding a state-of-the-art folding box plant next to two older plants that employed roughly 300 people. With the promise of jobs and tax revenues, Kraft's Rand-Whitney was awarded a permit to build the new facility, as well as improved road access and sewer hookups. But after the new plant was built, Rand-Whitney sold ownership of the two older plants to a company that in 1995 closed them down and laid off all 300 employees.

At the local Polish American Club, when the Patriots came on the TV, Sennott reported, "the old factory workers" rooted for the other team.

"The people in that Polish Hall don't know the facts," Kraft said. "It's like South Boston. They're uneducated." Kraft, a Columbia man, later claimed he meant "uneducated on the issues." But that's not what he said.

The stadium was already on life support. But when I saw that quote, I knew Kraft had pulled the plug.

And reading on, I knew Bill Weld would do nothing to help.

A truck driver had dropped off a package at Kraft's office and was waiting by the elevator. He was wearing a Green Bay Packers hat.

"Hey, do you know where you are?" Jonathan Kraft asked.

"I know exactly where I am and I know who works here," the man said. "And you can tell him he's never coming to South Boston so long as I live there."

The elevator doors closed. Jonathan "rolled his eyes" and said, "More of the riffraff."

Sennott asked me for a quote: "It's always hard for a business person to jump into the public arena. But this has been unbelievable."

The people of South Boston opposed the stadium because it would harm their neighborhood. The Krafts didn't get that. As I told Sennott, "They think everyone is against them." Jonathan Kraft wondered if it was because of anti-Semitism.

Three weeks after his damaging interview with Sennott, Bob Kraft generously took responsibility for "mishandling the whole affair, for not including community residents," and withdrew his proposal to build a football stadium in South Boston.

Foxboro officials said they would find a way to keep the team there.

And I said: Amen.

"Kraft's decision gives the mayor's development agenda a major boost," the *Globe* wrote. So long tied to the stadium, the convention center was free at last.

"Every day we wait on this, we lose another convention," I warned. Macworld, held in Boston for thirteen years, drawing fifty thousand visitors who spent $60 million in the city, was the latest. It had to be split between two sites in Boston. But the Javits Center, in New York, was big enough to host it at one site. In 1997, Macworld was Boston's biggest trade show. In 1998, Macworld announced it would switch to New York.

Forging ahead with the convention center still wasn't easy. In Massachusetts politics, nothing is.

To jump-start legislation on Beacon Hill, I proposed that the city buy the C Street land. Tom Finneran and I then wrangled for months over what Boston should pay. Minutes before the legislature was scheduled to debate the proposal, we settled on a price.

"While this is an important economic development project for the city and the state, no mayor in history has been willing to come up with a nickel to help fund it," Finneran said. "So Mayor Menino is to be congratulated for his willingness to commit the $157 million to make this new convention center a reality." I said nice things about him, too.

To win veto-proof approval of the $700 million bond issue to pay for the Boston Convention Center, legislators from across the state were cut in on the action. Southeastern Massachusetts got $30 million for capital projects; Fall River's Kerr Mill site $3.5 million; Worcester's convention center $17 million; Springfield's Basketball Hall of Fame $25 million and Civic Center $14 million; and Lenox, on the western border, $2.5 million for the National Music Center. With something for politicians from the Cape to the Berkshires, the bill passed, and by enough votes to override the governor's veto (because of the hike in the hotel tax).

In 1994 my BRA had selected the site, estimated the benefits, and specified the taxes to finance a convention center in South Boston. In 1998 construction began at C Street.

Stuff (finally!) had got done.

> We are facing some major challenges in Detroit. We're trying to reduce crime and build our neighborhoods, and we're here because we want to know what magic Mayor Menino is working.
>
> —*Detroit Mayor Dennis Archer, visiting Boston in January 2000*

Boston's recovery plan had a neighborhood component, the Main Streets initiative to revive community shopping districts by tapping "uncaptured spending power." That's econ-talk for a commonsense idea: Residents of even the poorest areas have money to spend, which goes uncaptured locally unless they have a safe place to shop. After 1995, the success of neighborhood policing began to change perceptions about neighborhood shopping. That was the first step in stimulating locally generated economic growth. The model describes a commercial chain reaction. Concentrated spending power attracts new businesses, which create new jobs, which support more spending, which attracts more businesses. I saw it happen in neighborhood after neighborhood.

Main Street is my baby. As a city councilor, I persuaded the National Trust for Historic Preservation to extend its Main Streets program, intended to revive commerce in rural America, to an urban commercial center. I had one in mind in my council district—Roslindale Square.

Angela remembers the square as a bustling place, with a drugstore that served ice cream sodas over a marble counter and a movie theater, the Rialto. One of the last movies to play there, in the early 70s, was a revival of *Gone with the Wind.* That's what happened to the square after the suburban malls captured the available spending power. In 1981 a four-alarm fire consumed a block of stores. Running for mayor in 1983, Dennis Kearney, the sheriff of Suffolk County, painted a dark picture for a Roslindale audience: "This year in Roslindale Square, there were eight auto thefts, nine burglaries and three armed robberies. Every candidate for mayor says Boston needs more jobs, but if you were opening a business, would you do it here?" Kearney lost big in Roslindale.

Campaigning for City Council that year, I tried the politics of hope. Speaking at a local Knights of Columbus hall, I said: "I have a master plan for Roslindale Square. We have to bring it back." I might not have been so positive if I had looked around. Walking through the square after my speech, I counted thirteen pizza joints.

I was on the advisory board of the National Trust for Historic Preservation and saw possibility for Roslindale in its National Main Street Center program, devised to revive rural village centers. My pitch was that cities were made up of villages. Roslindale Square even had a village green! Beneath the plywood faces of the shops were the bones of fine old buildings, constructed in the 1920s when Roslindale was a fashionable "streetcar suburb." The square could be renewed by uncovering — and recovering — its past. Like so much else in my career, now that I can see it whole, saving Roslindale Square was a back-to-the-future project.

The Trust went for my idea. In 1985 it made Roslindale Square an Urban Demonstration Project and awarded the Roslindale Main Street advisory board a grant of $100,000 annually for three years. The Trust promised "to bring those techniques successfully developed for stimulating economic development in small towns" to the square.

Working with a locally hired (and partly city-paid) director, Main Street consultants pursue a four-part strategy of "improving storefronts, streets and sidewalks; promoting the district to residents, investors and visitors; creating partnerships among neighborhood stakeholders; and advising existing merchants and recruiting new ones."

One piece of advice the consultants give: Lose the heavy metal grates, especially the pull-down kind that seal off the shop from the sidewalk. According to police, thieves who know they can't be seen from the front break in through the roof or from the back.

Signage is also critical. It's what people judge you by. Doors matter too. And rooflines. And the sides of buildings. The Main Street do-over focuses on aesthetics.

Revival happens slowly, one sign, one door, one new shop at a time. "You have to be patient because it's not going to turn around in just a year or two," said the president of the board of Roslindale Main Street. That piece of city wisdom echoes Tom Payzant on school reform: "It's painfully slow and very few urban school systems have been given the time."

I've been labeled "an incrementalist." A step-by-step mayor who resisted "bold dramatic change." But I didn't resist it. The city did. Cities do. Cities are complex social systems. Whether in the schools, public safety, housing, or neighborhood renewal, change is possible but in small pieces and in slow time.

Working for my degree in community planning at UMass Boston, one of my class projects was to estimate the benefits of implementing Main Streets in all city neighborhoods. By 1995, when I was mayor, the Roslindale experiment was so encouraging that realizing that project seemed possible. Boston Main Streets extended the model citywide.

Helping Roslindale fulfill its promise was my first priority. Four million dollars and untold volunteer hours were put into the renamed "Roslindale Village." By 2000, fifteen years after the first Main Street grant, these investments were paying off:

- The storefront vacancy rate had fallen from 20.7 percent to 3.5 percent.
- Forty-three commercial buildings were rehabbed, and the facades of seventy-three others renovated.
- Forty-four new businesses had opened, with two hundred employees.
- Sixty cents of every dollar spent in the village had stayed in the neighborhood.

In 2008, Roslindale Village became Boston's first commercial center to be rezoned as a twenty-first-century walkable business district. The new zoning discourages suburban big boxes separated from the street by parking lots. It bans drive-in businesses and stand-alone neon signs and, because they are unfriendly to pedestrians, limits curb cuts in the sidewalks for cars. Not zoning but self-interest has effectively banned "the ugly metal grates that made [the shops] look like five-and-dime fortresses." Merchants who refused to remove their grates forfeited Main Street grants.

If your taste runs that way, truffle cheese at $29 a pound can be had at one of the village's one-hundred-plus businesses. Or with three thousand other shoppers you can buy produce at the Saturday farmers' market held on the green. As a commercial hub, Roslindale Square was hollowed out in the 60s when local shoppers began driving to suburban malls. Today, suburbanites drive into Roslindale Village to dine at one of its trendy restaurants. The commuter rail "T" station, twelve minutes from downtown, is behind the village, steps from the stores. The Japanese man getting off the train may be a visiting mayor, scouting the future.

A journalist once marveled that I get excited about supermarkets. You bet your life I do! Like no other businesses, supermarkets tap local spending power. The eighteen-thousand-square-foot Village Market pulls customers into Roslindale Village. Landing it took years of work by the Main Street volunteers. Yours truly did his part, too, shooing away a national chain that wanted to fill the space it occupies. Years passed, and the gap on Corinth Street remained. It closed when the Village Market opened in 1998, starting a new chapter in the Roslindale story.

One of my tenets is that revival has to include not just the worst neighborhoods or the high-voting neighborhoods. That doesn't work: It doesn't make the city complete. So the Roslindale story is now playing out in eighteen other Main Street districts from Dorchester to East Boston. A city investment of $5.7 million in these commercial centers stimulated more than $40 million in private investment. The districts added 300 new businesses and 2,300 new jobs by 2000. Twelve years later, almost 1,000 businesses had been started up or expanded, 800 storefronts improved, and 6,000 jobs created.

Two quick examples:

- In the South End, the Washington Gateway Main Street organization received the Great American Main Street award in 2005 and the American Planning Association's Great Places in America award in 2008 for revitalizing urban blocks pocked for decades by unoccupied storefronts.
- Allston Village Main Streets is organized around an international theme, with sixty restaurants and markets featuring Greek, Brazilian, Russian, Korean, and Vietnamese food. On weekends new Americans share the crowded sidewalks with students from Boston University and Boston College. The district's website boasts: "Whether you're looking for pho or faux, suds or spuds, fish or Phish, carpets or car parts, you'll find it all in Allston Village." I can't get over the fact that this cool multicultural neighborhood emerged while a guy from Hyde Park was mayor.

At a 2000 conference sponsored by the National Trust for Historic Preservation, Boston's Main Streets program was singled out as a beacon of social innovation. "Boston is at the top," said Kennedy Smith, director of the Trust's Main Street Center. "It was the first city in the country to create a citywide, multidistrict approach, and now it's a model for other cities looking for solutions. We feel that it's one of the most dynamic and innovative new solutions for urban development to come along for several decades."

Commerce-led neighborhood revival breaks from the formula followed by community development corporations (CDCs) since the 60s — build subsidized housing first and retail will follow. It rarely did. I maintained that if small business districts didn't do well, neighborhoods wouldn't thrive. I was vice president of the U.S.

Conference of Mayors, which ensured that Boston's record with retail first got the attention of my colleagues. "Neighborhoods are hot right now, both in urban government and in politics," the editor of *Governing,* Alan Ehrenhalt, wrote in 2001. "Although not everyone realizes it, the phenomenon can be traced straight back to Boston."

Governing named me a Public Official of the Year, writing, "Menino is emerging as one of Boston's most influential chief executives, as his ideas begin to transform policy in cities far way." I was afraid it might be hard living up to the title the magazine gave me, "Main Street Maestro."

In the 60s cities turned to Washington to fund "urban renewal." Now Washington is broken. Given the destruction left behind by the federal bulldozer, perhaps it's just as well that the cavalry isn't coming and cities have to renew themselves. Boston Main Streets shows how.

> It was really almost a wasteland. What Menino accomplished there is not only a rebirth, but the complete refashioning of the entire area into what amounts to a new city.
>
> —*Howard Husock of the Manhattan Institute, describing Boston's new Innovation District*

Still, the question remained: Why build in Boston? Why build where building was so difficult? Where new projects had to submit cultural impact studies and run a gauntlet of fourteen review boards? Where, once they cleared the regulatory hurdles, developers were shaken down for multimillion-dollar "impact" and "linkage" fees to fund low-cost housing or job training?

In the booming 1980s Boston's reputation as a "place hostile to development" did not matter. "There was plenty of money on the table for all the deals," said Paul Barrett, a BRA director under Ray Flynn. For example, in the mid-80s the developer of an office tower on State Street paid for brick sidewalks around Faneuil Hall. But in the down economy of the early 90s, a $10 million renovation of a Downtown Crossing hotel was nixed because the "giveback" sought by the BRA was too steep.

A 1993 report prepared by Robert Walsh, BRA director in the late 70s, said Boston needed a developer-friendly approach to development. I endorsed the report as a candidate and implemented it as mayor.

Boston was "open for business," I declared in my first inaugural. "City government has acted as a gatekeeper to slow business down. . . . That will exist no more." The BRA taking four years to green-light a project downtown? No more. City Hall taking six weeks to grant a permit to rebuild a porch in the neighborhoods? No more.

In the first ten years of the century, according to figures published in the *Globe,* "Boston built more commercial space per square mile of land . . . than any of the nation's 10 most populous cities."

Besides guiding this building boom, my BRA updated the city's 1950s zoning code, rewrote the city's real estate development code to ease the regulatory burden on new projects, and designated sites where more development was wanted. All this was following Walsh, who spoke of the value for "both business and residents" of a streamlined, "predictable" review process.

But "predictable" is the last word my critics would apply to development in the Menino years. Kevin White, the downtown mayor, kept a "white-knuckled grip" on development. Ray Flynn, the "neighborhood mayor," left the big calls to his first BRA director, Steve Coyle. BRA directors can get lulled into thinking they head an independent agency. But if the mayor gives the nod, the board that rubber-stamped their hiring will rubber-stamp their firing. I had good directors, so-so ones, and a few flops. But I never relaxed my grip.

The press harped on the theme that I was afraid a powerful BRA chief would run against me for mayor. That wasn't it. I was hands-on because I thought city planning was too important to be left to the city planners.

Development was shot through with big issues and big headaches over favoritism, location, cost, height, and, yes, cultural impact. Upscale condos paid into a fund to build more affordable housing. Business projects paid for open space. In boom years we could ask them to pay more, but when the economy was bad we had to accept less. Decisions like these, and decisions on which projects to approve and which to reject, had to be made on a case-by-case basis, not through following a "predictable" one-size-fits-all approval process.

For example, Boston's zoning regulations permit flat roofs. But in Boston the mayor is stronger than the regulations, and he decides what gets built, where it gets built, when it gets built, who gets to build it, and how it gets built. And I didn't like flat roofs. In a widely publicized incident, a developer came to my City Hall conference room to show me a design for a high-rise in the Back Bay. I said no: It had a flat roof. He returned with a scale model and a dozen miniature tops and stuck one after another onto the building until I pointed to one I liked. An architecture critic called my top "a narcissistic crown" and sniffed that it "makes the building look like an ornamental perfume bottle." He can fix it when he's mayor.

I told developers: "I don't want sticks in the city anymore; sticks that go straight up to heaven. I want buildings with character." Where's the character in a flat roof?

A celebrated architect once compared himself to a whore for going through the motions on a Boston building in the 70s. I never wanted to read that about something built while I was mayor. So I put developers and architects on notice: Show me you know Boston from Oakland.

Developers who couldn't make the cut complained to reporters about the "Petty Thin-Skinned Ruthless S.O.B." in City Hall (a real headline). I poked fun at my bad rep. Raising money for a nonprofit, I appeared in a video dressed as the Godfather. An actor playing a developer I have no use for asks me, "What have I done that you would treat me with such disrespect?" And, stroking a stuffed cat, I tell him, "If you had come to me in friendship, your new tower would be up this very day."

I could laugh at my image as the don of development, but others saw nothing funny about it. "Never before in Boston, and perhaps nowhere else in the nation, has a mayor obsessed so mightily, and wielded power so exhaustively, over the look, feel, and shape of the built city," the *Globe* complained. "Routine construction projects on remote streets need City Hall approval; prominent towers that climb the downtown skyline carry his mark; independent city boards bow to his will." That guy sounds scary.

And ineffective. A mayor spread so thin would never get big stuff done, like "create a new neighborhood from whole cloth." That's how *Governing* summed up my effort to "reimagine the city's long disused waterfront as a new hub for high-tech firms and small start-ups, along with retail, housing, restaurants, and green space."

All along I had my eye on the waterfront. It had the potential to be Boston's first government-made neighborhood since the Back Bay was filled in after the Civil War. I was focused on that future when I opposed the megaplex and Bob Kraft's stand-alone stadium, both slated to be built in the then Seaport District. And I stayed focused on it while needling the mogul who ran a giant parking lot on the waterfront to develop the land or sell it to someone who would. He hung on year after year until forced to sell by a costly divorce. Then the recession hit. Finally, in my last inaugural in January 2010, I made standing up the Innovation District my top priority. Recession be damned.

"A new approach is called for on the waterfront," I declared at Faneuil Hall. "Together, we should develop these thousand acres into a hub for knowledge workers and creative jobs. . . . There has never been a better time for innovation to occur in urban settings than now, and there should be no better place than Boston."

Why Boston? Location, location, location. The Innovation District is just four subway stops away from MIT and Harvard and the Kendall Square biotechnological center billed (for now) as "the densest square mile of innovation on the planet."* *Governing* called my commitment to the Innovation District "perhaps the biggest gamble" of my career.

The gamble is paying off. Growth on the waterfront has surged. Using tax incentives, in a slow recovery, and with no help from Washington, we attracted several hundred new businesses with five thousand employees to move there. We asked entrepreneurs to help us start something new and they accepted our invitation.

The key: landing MassChallenge, Inc., "the world's largest startup accelerator." This one-of-a-kind nonprofit runs a competition for new businesses, connecting entrepreneurs with mentors, offering

* "Seemingly overnight Boston has become the new startup capital of the state's tech economy. . . . Last year, in fact, Boston accomplished a previously unheard of feat by having more venture capital deals than Cambridge — for years the center of gravity of the startup scene in Massachusetts." Kyle Alspach, "Boston Suddenly Finds Itself the State's Tech Startup Capital," *Boston Globe*, April 6, 2014.

free office space and help with finding investors. MassChallenge sowed a culture of collaboration in the district that, more than tax breaks, has brought in new ventures in biotech and green tech. MassChallenge changed people's ideas about the waterfront, and the waterfront is changing people's ideas about Boston.

The city mobilized private funding to build the twelve-thousand-square-foot Innovation Center, where tech workers and "bio-entrepreneurs" can exchange ideas and incubate new businesses. And Babson College, a leader in teaching entrepreneurship, is furnishing "hatchery space" for start-ups founded by its MBA students.

The culture of the Innovation District is also attractive to established knowledge industry companies like Vertex Pharmaceuticals, which sited its new global headquarters there. Its 1.1 million square feet of office space includes a three-thousand-square-foot laboratory where local students can conduct experiments beside Vertex scientists.

The Innovation District tries to live up to its name in housing, parking, and commuting.

"Everybody expects us to build high-rise condominiums, offices, and retail in the South Boston Waterfront; but that's Anywhere America," I said when calling for bids on vacant city-owned industrial buildings at the tip of the Innovation District. Instead, the idea is to promote live-work spaces, micro-apartments, and co-housing for professionals in the life sciences who expect turnkey Internet but are willing to share a kitchen. Developers must devote 15 percent of residential projects to living spaces modeled on "executive learning facilities" at Harvard and Babson that stimulate collaboration.

Work has begun on Seaport Square, a $3 billion project that will carve twenty new city blocks out of a wilderness of parking lots. A decade from now, five thousand people will live there, worship there, shop and dine there, stroll in two public parks there, go to the movies or the theater or a concert there.

On parking, the city has installed "smart parking sensors" along the neighborhood streets. Using a free mobile app, the sensors point motorists to open spaces. Information technology also eases the drive home: TIME TO DESTINATION signs wired to "real-time traffic data" help drivers find the quickest commute.

The Innovation District is "not the next Beacon Hill," says Mitch Weiss, a Harvard Business School grad and my last chief of staff. "It's linked to job clusters and a different kind of living" for highly educated young people living on modest budgets. Mitch sees the district, which he named, following a model in Barcelona, Spain, where scientists live within walking distance of their labs, so if the spirit moves them, they can return to work in the middle of the night.

"Geekville" rising on the South Boston peninsula: Who would have guessed it when I began my first term?

The question for the future is whether people living on modest budgets can afford to live in Boston, not just in the Innovation District.

"Prosperity brings its own challenges . . . and none is more acute than the region's severe housing crisis," notes a Boston Foundation study. Only New York and San Francisco have higher rents than Boston: $2.1 million is the median price of a single-family residence on Beacon Hill, in the Back Bay, and the South End, the city's skid row as recently as the 60s.

The average household income in Boston is $49,000. But in 2012–13 a couple earning $75,000 could afford only 5 percent of houses sold in Charlestown, 7 percent in South Boston, and 15 percent in Jamaica Plain. In 2005 the Economic Policy Institute found Greater

Boston "the most expensive place to live in the country." It hasn't got any cheaper since.

Alan Ehrenhalt, a leading urban affairs journalist, sees a "Great Inversion" in American living patterns. After decades when families moved out of the city as they moved up the class ladder, "people who possessed money and choice were increasingly living in the center, while newcomers and the poor were settling in the suburbs, often in the outer reaches of suburban territory." And as suburban empty nesters move into the city, they bid up housing prices beyond anything longtime residents can pay. Rich foreigners are doing the same thing to luxury housing.

I sometimes ask myself: Did the mayors who transformed Boston from "a hopeless backwater, a tumbled-down has-been among cities"—Hynes, Collins, White, Flynn, Menino—succeed too well? Is Boston too attractive to the well heeled and the well educated? On Boston's four-hundredth birthday in 2030, will the city have a place for an ambitious worker like Carl Menino? For a plugger good with numbers like me? Or will Boston then look like Paris now, a city for the elite ringed by suburbs for those who cater to them?

Cities can recharge their own economies. We proved that in Boston. But what can cities do to reverse the greatest threat to social hope in America, economic inequality? Today, you want to live the American Dream? Go to Canada. Upward mobility is greater there (and in class-ridden Great Britain) than in the USA.

Against inequality, cities do what can be done—pass living wage ordinances, for example—not all that *needs* to be done. Legislation to address inequality must come from Washington. The first New Deal built a foundation of economic security for the industrial age. It's time for a second New Deal for the information age.

We are not moving back to a future of good jobs for people of good character at the Westinghouse plant. "Dependable" won't take you very far in a global economy. The values I learned from Carl and Susan Menino don't predict success in life in today's knowledge society nearly as well as getting the right grades from the right schools. And neither counts for as much as "winning the ovarian lottery," to quote Warren Buffett. By age four, a child born into an affluent family has heard 15 million more words than a child from a poor family. How can we reconcile that gap with the American ideal of "equal opportunity"?

The good news is that in the New America of hardening class inequality, city government can redistribute tax revenue from the affluent to the struggling, from neighborhoods where people own to neighborhoods where they rent.

I recently saw an ad for a Federal-era mansion for sale on Beacon Hill. Price: $10 million. Besides trimming their trees and collecting their rubbish, Beacon Hill residents ask little from City Hall. So with the $60,000 collected yearly in property taxes on that house, the city can pay for public goods like parks and playgrounds for kids in Roxbury, Dorchester, and Mattapan. Also housing, libraries, cultural programs, mass transportation, a clean environment, and health care. Boston ranks just behind New York as the most unequal city in the country, but by providing the money for these goods, Boston's growing wealth can benefit the whole community.* The city can leverage economic inequality to strengthen social equality. To make it so that, in Boston, you don't have to be rich to have a rich life.

* "We've been able to do something that none of these other cities can do, and that is attract a lot of the very wealthy from around the country and the world. . . . And they're the ones that pay a lot of the taxes. . . . And we take tax revenue from those people to help people throughout the entire rest of the spectrum. And you know, it gives you this income-inequality measure." New York Mayor Michael Bloomberg on his weekly radio show, September 20, 2013.

"HEYHOWAYA?"

> The critiques of Menino—that he gets too much credit just for showing up, that his administration is too secretive and insular, that his record of improving life in the neighborhoods is exaggerated—have begun to resonate, thanks to constant repetition, and a steady drip of bad news emanating from the mayor's suite.
>
> —*from a* Boston Globe *editorial during the 2009 campaign*

I've tried to keep the brag down in this book, citing facts or others' opinions. But for once take my word for it: I was not a crook. I ran a clean government. The city's lawyers cautioned me to proceed carefully against employees under a cloud: They might sue. I spurned that advice. At the first hint of corruption, appointees were out the door. Employees with civil service protection were harder to fire, but I made life miserable for them.

A reporter preparing a story on my temper once asked if it was true that I ran City Hall like "a drill sergeant." I didn't deny it. "I expect the best out of my people," I said. "I demand it sometimes. The public demands it of me all the time."

People believed I'd do the right thing for the city. Abuse their trust, and I'd spend my time trying to regain what I'd lost. I'd get nothing done. Keeping the public trust applied in spades to my own conduct. The only check on Boston's emperor/mayor was the emperor/mayor. It was up to me to keep me in line.

Mostly I succeeded. In 2000 I pledged not to take political contributions from developers with business before the city: "What you're talking about is my integrity, and there is absolutely no price on that." Partly because aides were competing to see who could raise the most *money, that promise was broken, and I wound up accepting donations from a few such developers, some of which we returned. The amount came to a paltry $10,000 out of more than $5 million raised from other sources. When an investigative reporter told me that six "pet" developers with no pending business before the city had contributed $61,000 over four years, I commented: "That's all? Cheap bums."*

The issue of public ethics involved is this: Did I practice "pay for play" by favoring developers who made donations over those who didn't? Donations did not determine my decisions. They were one among many factors. My "pet" developers had track records of outstanding performance. Norman Leventhal, a Dorchester paperboy who became a great Boston benefactor, once came into my office and began to describe a new project. "Don't tell me where it is, Norman," I interrupted. "Just build it." That's how much I trusted him.

Contributions aside, what about personal connections? Suppose you had to choose between a proposal from a friend and one from a stranger. Other things being equal, you'd do what I did. You'd favor the friend. Voters are human too. They cut you more slack over friends than over money. (I make no apologies for a 2001 decision that combined them: stopping a chain drugstore from opening near a pharmacy owned by a friend and contributor.)

Corruption is one of two reasons voters fire incumbents. I was safe on that front. The other reason is they want change. There I was vulnerable. In 2009 I had been mayor for sixteen years. Maybe I was kidding myself, but I wanted another term to improve people's lives.

This is the story of my closest election.

I knew it would be a tough year in January, when, in my State of the City speech, I addressed the hard times brought on by the Wall Street crash: "We are confronting a great economic crisis. Boston did not create it. But Boston must deal with it. . . . Whether it's at your kitchen table, or my desk, the numbers are not pretty." To make up a $140 million budget shortfall, I said, unions representing city employees had to choose: a wage freeze or layoffs. "The mayor is popular now, but will he be popular after he lays off hundreds of teachers, cops, and firefighters?" asked the Globe. New initiatives? Forget about it. Holding the line on existing services would be a miracle.

One observer called the speech "the most dour assessment of the state of the city since British troops roamed Roxbury."

In my two earlier contested races, 2001 and 2005, I did not run TV ads until the last week in October, and they were jokey productions. In 2009 I started running ads in April, and they were serious.

A second hurdle to my reelection was "Menino fatigue." People had to be tired of seeing me on TV. The financial crisis ruled out running on a bold vision for my precedent-shattering fifth term. I always want to look ahead, to talk about tomorrow. But reality would force me to look back, reminding voters of what I'd done in the past. In the run-up to the preliminary election in September, that would play into the strategy of my two challengers: to style me as yesterday's mayor.

"He works hard but this race will not be about the past 16 years but about the next four years," declared one challenger. His campaign slogan was "A New Season for Boston." I was an "old school Sony Walkman" mayor. He'd be an "iPod" mayor. He was forty.

The other challenger hit the same note: "It's time to bring in a new generation of leadership." His slogan was "A New Way of Politics." Appearing "so boyish he looks like he needed to get a parent's permission slip for a field trip," he was thirty-nine.

I ran on the slogan "Moving Boston Forward." But my vow to reach *out to the "generation that gave us Facebook" looked silly when the press reported that I resisted voice mail.* I was sixty-six.*

I couldn't hide how sour I was over the Gramps treatment:

REPORTER: *Which candidate poses the greater threat to you?*
ME: *I'm not going to pick one over the other.*
REPORTER: *Which would you rather grab a beer with?*
ME: *I don't drink.*

Challenger One was City Councilor at-Large Michael Flaherty of South Boston. The top vote-getter in three straight council elections and council president for five years. I'd backed him for the job. I'd hoped for loyalty but counted on patience, figuring Mike was young enough to wait out one more Menino term.

"I'd been advised to wait," Mike said in one speech. "I said, 'The city can't wait.' For . . . mothers I've met over the course of this campaign who have lost their sons to senseless violence, I say, we can't wait. For children across the city who dropped out of the Boston public schools or who currently are in underperforming schools, I say we can't wait."

After he got 50,000 votes running for reelection in 2005, 14,000 short of my total that year, it was clear that he wasn't likely to wait. So I backed another councilor for president.

Challenger Two was At-Large City Councilor Sam Yoon, a Korean American community organizer funded by a national network of Asian American contributors. To win his seat in 2005, he'd defeated four Irish American candidates, among them the son of a former

* It was true. I didn't want citizens calling City Hall to talk to a machine. I'm told voice mail is considered a "blocking technology" anyway. In my last term, spurred by my tech-savvy chief of staff, Mitch Weiss, the city adopted "engagement technology" like Citizen Connect, a mobile app allowing people to send in photographs of potholes, graffiti, and broken streetlights and track the response to their complaints.

mayor, the daughter of another, and the son of a former secretary of state of the Commonwealth. Yoon was a classically trained pianist who attended "logic camp" as a kid. A Princeton grad. The holder of an advanced degree from Harvard. A newcomer to Boston. The face of the majority-minority city.

With his résumé, it was no surprise that Yoon demanded debates. "For us not to begin immediately to debate shortchanges the voters of Boston," he said. "There is too much at stake right now, with this economy and this budget crisis, for us not to be talking to the public about our platform and vision." Flaherty, a former prosecutor, also clamored for debates. At a City Hall press conference, when reporters badgered me on the subject, I grew testy. "We'll debate the issues," I said. "Did you hear what I say? We'll debate the issues. Next one? Do I have to repeat that line again? We'll debate the issues that face the city." And this was only April!

"He welcomes debates as much as a colonoscopy," wrote one columnist.

At a political roast my eloquence came in for ribbing. "As you know, I'm running for mayor of Boston, and I have an opponent," Flaherty began. "My opponent works very hard, is highly educated, and is known to speak a foreign tongue. . . . Councilor Yoon, welcome to the mayor's race." Congressman Stephen Lynch said he had heard from President Obama the day after I joined other mayors at a White House meeting: "The president wanted to make a point of how impressed he was with the mayor. He said, 'Congressman, I had no idea that your mayor speaks English as a second language.'" I even got into the act. "Writing books is a new thing for local pols," I said. "[State Representative] Brian Wallace wrote one, the governor is working on his. I'm starting mine. It's called the Menino-to-English dictionary."

• • •

The media was billing it as "the most competitive mayoral race in a generation" even before, a week after the September preliminary, the campaign took a dramatic turn.

Yoon was eliminated in the preliminary, placing third with 21 percent of the vote. With Flaherty getting 24 percent to my 50 percent, it looked like I'd cruise to victory in the November final. Flaherty's Old Boston background had little appeal to Yoon's New Boston voters.

Then Flaherty made what one columnist called a "big league move . . . to recast the campaign dynamic." He announced a political partnership with Sam Yoon. Flaherty promised to appoint Yoon as his chief adviser under the title of deputy mayor. Standing with his new partner on City Hall Plaza, an energized Flaherty declared: "There's a real race for mayor, folks, in Boston. It starts today." Flaherty embraced Yoon's call for term limits to "put an end to the 'mayor for life' culture that has held Boston back."

The op-ed writers were ecstatic. The pairing was "a bold—and potentially winning—gambit." "The race is shaping up as a real choice between old and new." "Flaherty's grounded understanding of Boston politics and Yoon's desire to modernize city management could complement each other well—combining their insider and outsider critiques of Menino."

"Floon is real," Flaherty said, using the media's shorthand for his combo with Yoon. "We have gay marriage here in Boston. We also have a great political marriage."

The two campaigned together. They appeared in ads together. They even coordinated their wardrobes. "Today, I just feel like wearing a sweater," Flaherty texted Yoon. "How about you?"

"What do you mean 'ticket'?" I shouted over the phone at a reporter. "Just one name is going to be on the ballot, and that's Mike Flaherty." There was no such title as "deputy mayor" in the city charter. It was a blatant attempt to confuse the voters.

Just when I needed some good press, the media discovered "E-gate," a non-scandal involving one of my closest aides. State law requires public officials not to erase their emails. But, thinking they were being saved by the system, he had erased over five thousand of his. Flaherty seized on the missing emails to denounce "sixteen years of autocratic rule."

Stories appeared about my powerful machine. "Dozens, even hundreds," of city workers by day were said to be taking names at Floon rallies by night. A Charlestown barber claimed one of my operatives pressured him to quit Flaherty's Facebook group. When, at a candidates' forum in Roxbury, a woman ignored a no-applause rule to clap every time I spoke, Flaherty asked me, "How many city workers did you bring tonight?" Yoon volunteers complained that city inspectors had cited the campaign for having too many signs in the window of Yoon's Field's Corner office. A Yoon aide told a reporter that you couldn't trust polls of Boston voters "because Boston city workers — and there are 20,000 of them — will lie to pollsters out of fear that if they let slip anything less than full-throated support of the mayor, it'll get back to the boss . . . the sort of omnipotence usually reserved for Kim Jong Il."

I struck back at the story line that made me an autocrat (Kim Jong Il!) and Flaherty the good government candidate, charging at one debate, "I think it's jobs for votes — telling Sam Yoon, 'You have a job in my administration if I win,' hoping to get Sam Yoon's votes for Mike Flaherty." Commentators hit on this theme, one writing: "So let me see if I have this straight. Sam Yoon gets promised a job in exchange for an endorsement. And this is the reform movement?"

Boston Firefighters Local 718, my old nemesis, endorsed Flaherty, and attacked me in ugly ads that Flaherty refused to watch, let alone denounce. One showed an elderly lady sprawled on the floor beside her walker. The voice-over said firefighters would usually answer 911 calls within four minutes — "But only if your emergency call is on the mayor's list." The visual changed to a shot of me, the cur refusing to raise firefighters' pay 20 percent in exchange for drug testing. I'd been pushing testing for two years, ever since two firefighters were killed in a West Roxbury fire and cocaine was found in one man's body and alcohol in the other's. Another ad charged that my administration "had contributed to the death of Kevin Kelly," a firefighter killed when the brakes on his fire truck failed. Former mayor Ray Flynn piled on, recording an ad blaming me for faulty maintenance, lousy equipment, and terrible morale among firefighters.

When he wasn't promising the moon to Local 718 — by agreeing to create an unnecessary hazmat unit to bleed overtime pay, for example — Mike Flaherty was repeating "sixteen years."

- *"The mayor has had sixteen years to fix the schools. I'd say that's enough."*
- *"This is a different city and a different economy, and we're not going to be able to solve today's problems with 16-year-old ideas."*
- *"More than 1,000 people have been murdered in Boston over the past sixteen years."*
- *"The mayor will say anything to stand in the way of progress, of innovation, of good ideas. That's what [Boston] has had to bear with this last 16 years."*

But my longevity was a double-edged sword. One man's Menino fatigue was another man's Menino familiarity. A poll taken during the campaign found that 54 percent of the city's population claimed to have met me. Put another way, over those sixteen years I'd said "Heyhowaya?" to around 256,000 Bostonians. Most I'd encountered once. But others . . .

When a reporter asked a woman sitting with friends at an East Boston Dunkin' Donuts "to list all the places she has run into Menino, she quickly listed five and stopped with a look that said, how long should I go on?"

Asked if she knew me, another random woman, Thelma Henderson, eighty-three, of Roxbury, said: "That's my man. He looks after me. He stopped by my house to make sure I was comfortable during the hot days."

At a Christmas tree lighting ceremony during my last month in office, a man introduced himself and said we'd never met before. "Where have you been?" I asked him.

My model of governing called for me to be out of City Hall listening to citizens at Christmas tree lightings, pancake breakfasts, groundbreakings, ribbon cuttings . . . Critics said I'd attend the opening of an envelope.

Tell me Monday about a pothole on your street, and it would be filled by Friday or I'd know why not. A politician can expect no higher praise than "He kept his promises." In the grand scheme of things, perhaps filling a pothole doesn't matter. But to the citizen who nearly lost a tire in that pothole, it says, "You matter."

The human factor. It's everything in politics. In 2012 Governing *magazine said I set the model for twenty-first-century mayors. My portable formula: Do the small stuff—fix potholes, clean up parks, plow the streets quickly after snowstorms—to win the public's trust that you'll deliver on the big stuff.*

The last question in the campaign's last debate was, Should city workers retire at sixty-five? I broke out in a grin. "I don't believe in mandatory retirement," I said. Neither did the voters. I won by 15 points.

I was disappointed. I was hoping for 16.

Chapter 5

"To Think I Did All That . . ."

> He leaves office . . . having presided over and facilitated one of the most successful urban renaissance stories in modern American history.
>
> — New York Times, *January 5, 2014*

NO SOONER HAD I given my victory speech after winning a fifth term than commentators began speculating about the odds of a sixth. "It is almost inconceivable that Menino will run again in 2013," a *Globe* editorial predicted. "Like a much-loved 1950s Chevy, his reelection machine can now be packed away."

No way would I follow that advice. Keeping my reelection machine tuned up was in the city's interest. If I packed the old Chevy away, I'd get less money for affordable housing from builders of upscale condominiums, and I'd have less weight with employers deciding between staying in Boston or going out of town.

I wanted the boys in the boardrooms whispering: *This guy might be mayor for life. We can't afford to tick him off. The mayor of Boston is an elected emperor. He can do whatever the hell he wants. Me-*

nino? He's a thin-skinned emperor. Make him angry and he'll make us pay. Paul Grogan, the president of the Boston Foundation, nailed it: "People spend an enormous amount of time thinking about how to please him and how not to piss him off." Restaurant owners who get on Hizzoner's bad side — it's easy to do — receive "constant underwear checks" by city inspectors. Politicians who oppose him become nonpersons. Take Sam Yoon. After running against Menino in '09, he was "radioactive." Employers were afraid to give him a job. He lived off credit cards for months, and to find work, he had to pull up stakes and head to Washington. Menino freezes out journalists who criticize him. Take Larry Harmon. The mayor dipped into a fund intended to beautify the city in order to buy charm bracelets for departing staffers, and Larry wrote a piece slamming him for it. Afterward, Larry says Dot Joyce told him, "The mayor will never speak to Larry Harmon again." The third person. Like a sentence of doom from Mordor. Remember Kobie, the gorilla who pelted Menino with his shit? Well, as Harmon tells it, "a few months later, Kobie died of complications from anesthesia during his annual physical exam. That was the official explanation, at least."

Fear is power. I owed it to my city to keep fear alive.

Look what happened when Partners HealthCare knew they didn't have to answer to me anymore. In my last year we were in discussions with Partners, which runs Mass General and Brigham and Women's hospitals, about consolidating its scattered administrative operations by moving four thousand of its employees to a site near Roxbury's Dudley Square. Its neighbors there, Madison Park Technical Vocational High School and Roxbury Community College, could design courses to fit Partners' job requirements, starting local minority kids on an upward path in life. Their teachers could promise them, "Work hard today, and tomorrow you can have a career in information technology, finance, medical record keeping, and software services right over there, in that new office building." The kids would see hope out the window.

I announced I would not run for a sixth term in March. Partners waited until after the election of a new mayor, Martin J. Walsh, in November, to make an announcement of its own, timed to the political sweet spot between Menino and Walsh.

Moving jobs to Roxbury, Partners concluded, was just too expensive. Instead, thousands of its Boston employees would be sent to an upscale $1.5 billion mega-development in the adjacent city of Somerville, with the likes of Brooks Brothers, Le Creuset French cookware, and Legoland Discovery Center as its neighbors. I called the rejection of Roxbury a "disgrace." Partners had lost its "social conscience." The cost argument I dismissed. If taxed at the going commercial rate, Partners would pay $92 million a year on its nearly $3 billion worth of tax-exempt property in the city instead of leaving Boston a tip of $14 million. Any cost comparison of Roxbury versus Somerville should include that great deal. Partners' bottom-line decision, the *Globe* editorialized, "violate[d] the spirit of its privileged tax status."

The 3,700 jobs leaving Boston, Partners' aborted move to Roxbury—both were consequences of my retirement. For, as Larry Harmon observed, "it's safe to assume that Partners would have warmed up to the parcel in Roxbury if Menino had been sticking around for another four years. After all, he understands power and how to wield it to help the city's poor."

Partners times ten would have been the story of my last term if I had done what the *Globe* suggested and made myself a lame duck from day one.

> What is . . . vision? Sometimes we get caught up in the grandiose. My vision is jobs, a better school system, community

> policing, health care. When I leave this job, I want the city to be in better shape than when I took it over.
>
> —*from a 1994 interview*

I also owed it to my city to retire. My effectiveness as a leader depended on being "out there," where people expected to see me. And in my fifth term, out there, in the neighborhoods, my presence was missed. That much-cited 2009 poll found that 57 percent of Boston's 450,000 adult residents had personally met me. In a March 2013 poll, only 49 percent made that claim.

In the 1960s, John F. Collins governed Boston for eight years from a wheelchair. Being on the scene, listening, absorbing information, and responding to complaints, in short, doing the urban mechanic's job — that was not Mayor Collins's bond with the people. It was mine. The spirit was willing, but my flesh was weak.

Five days after my 2009 victory speech, I stumbled walking upstairs at my son's house and severed the tendon in my left knee. Over the years my health had not been great. I'd had a bout with a rare cancer. I was diagnosed with Crohn's disease, an inflammatory bowel condition. I had high blood pressure. I was overweight. But after that bum knee, everything seemed to go wrong. I delivered the State of the City address in January 2010 with my leg in a cast. For the next four years I was rarely seen in public without a cast or cane. After falling in the shower, I was hospitalized with an infected elbow and readmitted after experiencing a bad reaction to antibiotics. I needed surgery to repair a torn tendon in my right knee. I suffered a broken toe.

In October 2012, Angela and I left Boston for a two-week cruise in Italy. I'd been feeling under the weather, but couldn't cancel a trip that she'd planned for three years to mark our forty-sixth wedding anniversary. (Imagine the headline: "Mayor Gets Divorced.") On the cruise ship I got sicker and sicker. I lost all my energy. Turns out I'd developed a blood clot in my leg that traveled to my lungs. Back in Boston, doctors at Brigham and Women's diagnosed me with a severe respiratory infection. As I was about to be released, I suffered a compression fracture in a vertebra of my spine. When an unusual infection developed near it, doctors discovered I had type 2 diabetes. I spent five weeks at the Spaulding Rehabilitation Hospital recovering from my month-long stay at the Brigham.

My health caused strain, stress, and worry for my family and staff. Yet despite everything, I got big things done in my fifth term. I discussed one of them in Chapter 4 — standing up the Innovation District. But the critical developments came in politics. By using my field organization to get out the vote for candidates for state and national office, I banked political capital, and in term five I spent it to get important legislation through the State House.

Crushing Boston majorities helped elect the first black governor in the history of the Commonwealth, Deval Patrick, in 2006, and the first woman senator, Elizabeth Warren, in 2012.

For Warren, running against a popular Republican incumbent, Scott Brown, we pulled out all the stops. I asked Michael Kineavy, my political guru since 1993, to organize the Warren campaign in Boston. Scores of employees from the Boston Housing Authority, the Transportation Department, the Office of Neighborhood Services, and other city agencies took vacation time to staff the machine. Our 2,289 volunteers knocked on 117,000 doors. Our sound truck specialists got together with our foreign-language specialists, and soon voters in selected wards were being blasted with pitches for Warren and President Obama in Spanish, Cape Verdean Creole, Vietnamese, and other languages. On Election Day, our network of "foot pullers," "closers," sign holders, and van drivers helped mobilize 251,339 voters, Boston's largest turnout since 1964. Three out of four voted for Warren.

In national politics, in the 2008 presidential primary in Massachusetts, my people delivered for Hillary Clinton. A month earlier, when her candidacy hung in the balance, one hundred of our campaign pros camped out in Manchester, New Hampshire, to put Hillary over the top in the New Hampshire primary.

Democratic state legislators in Massachusetts drew a lesson from our wins: For those considering a run for higher office (all of them), the road to victory led through Boston. "Team Menino" could make you or break you. (I withheld support from a Democratic gubernatorial candidate in the 90s, and he lost Boston and the race by 42 points.)

Political clout helped me win passage of two bills that benefited cities and towns across the Commonwealth. I discussed one in Chapter 2. It allowed cities to create "in-district" charter schools that combined the flexibility of regular charters with control by local school boards. The second bill overhauled public pensions. Among other reforms, it repealed a provision that allowed firefighters claiming career-ending injuries while filling in for a superior to collect a disability pension at a higher pay grade. For Democratic legislators, elected with campaign contributions from the firefighters' union, ending this "king-for-a-day" rip-off was a tough vote.

Even as I got big stuff done, the quality of my face time with residents deteriorated. On the occasions when I did get "out there," people were too nervous about jarring my cane to crowd around me, which left me frustrated that I couldn't connect in the old way. "You're not enjoying this, Mayor, are you?" Dot asked in the van returning from an event. I wasn't.

It was time to go. Yet, hoping for a return of my old energy, and to preserve my power, I could not let go.

"Our future is bright," I said in my last State of the City address. In the "era of the city, Boston is the city of the era." The eight-hundred-strong audience gave me a standing ovation. Andrew Ryan, the *Globe* City Hall reporter, clocked it at two minutes, forty-six seconds. It was a long good-bye.

I outlined an ambitious agenda: using 1 million square feet of city property to build affordable housing, increasing the school budget by $30 million to pay for a longer school day, welcoming sixty-eight new police recruits. I put forward my proposal to make "Boston the premier city for working women." Handicappers took that as a hint I was running: a bid for the women's vote.

"This week, as Tom Menino gave his State of the City Address, Boston politicos scrutinized him carefully for signs that might foretell an end to his 20-year reign," wrote a reporter for the *Boston Phoenix,* an "alternative" weekly. "Clues were presumed to lie somewhere in the mayor's rehabilitated legs, infected respiratory system, still-healing back, diabetic blood, Crohn's-diseased intestines, or recently clotted lungs. . . . But the body parts holding the answer to this year's mayoral election might be John Connolly's balls."

Connolly was an at-large city councilor. When I was first elected mayor, he was a student at Harvard. In appearance he was Sam Yoon II: another thirty-nine-year-old who looked like he didn't shave.

Other potential candidates were holding off to see if I would run. "If the mayor decides not to seek another term, I'm absolutely going to be running," boldly declared Representative Marty Walsh. Connolly was gearing up to run regardless. "I'm not making this decision based on what the mayor does," he told reporters, while still mulling. "I'm making this decision because I think I can bring about real change in our schools and bring a new generation of leadership to City Hall." But were his body parts up to the challenge of taking me on?

The answer came on March 23. In the same room at the Parker House where John F. Kennedy launched his first campaign for Congress, John Connolly announced his candidacy. He hit hard at the schools. Four years earlier, Mike Flaherty's refrain was "sixteen years." Now Connolly's was "twenty."

- For "twenty years," elementary school kids had no access to art, music, science, you name it.
- For "twenty years," Boston had among the country's shortest school days.
- For "twenty years," high school students had not been prepared for college.

Twenty years of effort, millions spent. The result? "An abject failure."

"I think Mayor Menino is a good man whom I immensely respect," Connolly said. Then he handed me a gold watch: "But I don't think our schools will change without new ideas, new energy, and new leadership."

What did I think of Connolly? reporters asked. "A nice young man," I said.

Connolly's attack on the schools riled me ("Look at the improvements we've made . . ."). I sounded eager to climb back into the ring against the whippersnapper: "Let's have a . . . good campaign. Let's discuss the issues, the real issues."

Did my "use of the present tense" indicate I was running? reporters asked.

"I'm ready," I said.

Are you announcing now? asked WBZ-TV reporter Bill Shields.

"Shields, go back to the Cape," I said, laughing.

"On a scale of one to 10, I think it's a 10 he's running again," said Mike McCormack, that veteran of Boston politics. "And if he runs, I think he'll win."

The *Globe* commissioned a survey of Boston voters to find out. "If Menino ran again, he would probably win handily, but I think there's a desire among a lot of people to have a new mayor," the pollster commented. "It's not that they are unhappy with Menino, voters just think it's time for new blood at the top." The poll's finding that I'd beat Connolly by 29 points made it easier for me to do the necessary.

I faced it all and I stood tall . . .
—from "My Way"

Even as I bantered with the press about running, I prepared for the moment of truth. I had until five P.M. on May 13 to apply for nomination papers, the first step toward getting my name on the ballot, but I'd waited long enough.

A week in advance, Dot arranged with the International Brotherhood of Electrical Workers to rent Faneuil Hall for the afternoon of March 28, and the IBEW pulled city permits for a health care rally. The union was our disguise; nobody suspected. The night before, I called friends and colleagues with the news.

"I might change my mind at four o'clock, you never know," I said the next morning to reporters waiting in front of my house. "I may say something different and pull a Kevin White." In a payback for years of attacks, Kevin leaked word to the *Boston Herald* that he was running for reelection as mayor in 1983 the day before he announced he wasn't running.

The evening I became acting mayor, July 12, 1993, neighbors celebrated with a cookout, and Angela and I danced to Sinatra's "My Way" playing on a loudspeaker set out on a front porch. It was playing again on March 28, 2013, as Angela and I inched down the center aisle of Faneuil Hall, acknowledging applause, squeezing hands, and greeting old friends, some fighting back tears. I teared up myself when I saw my grandkids, all born while I was mayor, standing on the stage, waiting for their "Papa." They were clapping but not inside. My decision to retire . . . the hardest part was telling Giulia, Olivia, Will, Samantha, Taylor, and Thomas III.

"I never dreamed I would end up here: Mayor of Boston during its best days," I began my short speech. "Jobs, graduation ratings, construction, credit ratings are all at record highs. Population, school enrollment, crime rates, and housing all have hit their best mark in years. . . . Most important to me, we are now a more open and accepting city. It was a new day when you picked a Mayor with Italian grandparents. It's a much newer day now.

"Over the past few months, I have been weighing my own place in Boston's bright future. . . . I have been blessed to regain so much of my health.

"I am back to a Mayor schedule, but not a Menino schedule.

"And I miss that. I miss hitting every event, ribbon cutting, new homeowner dinner, school play, and chance meeting. Spending . . . time in the neighborhoods gives me energy."

Then I voiced Menino's urban mechanic theory of government: "Being with our residents builds our trust. It may not be the only way to lead Boston, but it's the only way for me.

"So I am here with the people I love, to tell the city I love, that I will leave the job that I love. I can run, I can win, and I can lead, but not as 'in-the-neighborhoods-all-the-time' as I like."

Nineteen years had gone by since I first spoke from that stage as mayor of Boston, since I said, "I'm not a fancy talker," since I called the roll of my Hyde Park ghosts, since in my mind's eye I saw my kid self chasing JFK's limo toward the last rally of that long-ago campaign. Nineteen years. I still could not get over my rise, one of the most unlikely stories in American politics. Maybe you feel the same way. How did this guy do it? I haven't a clue. No. That's not right. I have one clue.

America in my years was still a democratic society. A Harry Truman, a Ronald Reagan, a Bill Clinton, a Barack Obama, even a Tom Menino could rise from humble circumstances to the top. I made the most of my tryout as acting mayor. I showed I could do the job. I had a chance. I hope we can remain a country where people like me have a chance.

In the audience I saw members of my team who had made me look good for decades. I'd land on my feet, but I worried about them. How could I begin to thank them? They were as amazed as I was at how far we had come. To think, I said, that "thirty years ago, when I first ran for office, my father Carl worried I would end up unemployed. Instead, my neighbors put their trust in me." Whether I proved worthy of it is for others to say.

Two weeks later, entering a school in Dorchester, I fell and broke my right leg. Three days after that, the bombs went off at the Marathon. Standing in the pulpit at the interfaith service, I recalled the scenes that moved a nation. What people saw, I said, was the generous spirit of the great city whose service was my life. "We love the brave ones who felt the blast and still raced to the smoke. With ringing in their ears, they answered the cries of those in need. . . . We love the fathers who took the shirts off their backs to stop the bleeding, the mothers and sisters who cared for the injured. . . . The neighbors and the business owners, the homeowners all across the city, [who] opened their doors and their hearts to the weary and the scared. They said, what's mine is yours. We'll get through this together. . . . We have never loved the people of the city . . . more. . . . Nothing can defeat the heart of this city. Nothing. Nothing will take us down because we take care of one another. Thank you."

Index

Index